Thomas Cook **traveller** guides

CALABRIA
Lara Dunston & Terry Carter

Your travelling companion since 1873

Thomas
Cook

Written by Lara Dunston and Terry Carter, updated by Zoë Ross
Original photography by Terry Carter

Published by Thomas Cook Publishing
A division of Thomas Cook Tour Operations Limited
Company registration no. 3772199 England
The Thomas Cook Business Park, Unit 9, Coningsby Road,
Peterborough PE3 8SB, United Kingdom
Email: books@thomascook.com, Tel: + 44 (0) 1733 416477
www.thomascookpublishing.com

Produced by Cambridge Publishing Management Limited
Burr Elm Court, Main Street, Caldecote CB23 7NU
www.cambridgepm.co.uk

ISBN: 978-1-84848-390-3

First edition © 2009 Thomas Cook Publishing
This second edition © 2011
Text © Thomas Cook Publishing
Maps © Thomas Cook Publishing/PCGraphics (UK) Limited

Series Editor: Karen Beaulah
Production/DTP: Steven Collins

Printed and bound in Spain by GraphyCems

Cover photography © Travel Library Limited/Superstock

Contents

Background   4–19
Introduction   4
Land and people   6
History   10
Politics   12
Culture   14
Festivals and events   18

Highlights   20–25
Highlights   20
Suggested itineraries   22

Destination guide   26–119
Reggio di Calabria province   26
Vibo Valentia province   52
Catanzaro province   70
Cosenza province   76
Crotone province   110

Getting away from it all 120–25

Practical guide   126–57
When to go   126
Getting around   128
Accommodation   130
Food and drink   132
Entertainment   136
Shopping   140
Sport and leisure   144
Children   148
Essentials   150
Emergencies   156

Directory   158–73

Index   174–5

Maps
The land   9
Highlights   20
Reggio di Calabria province   27
Walk: Reggio di Calabria   33
Drive: Parco Nazionale
    dell'Aspromonte   49
Vibo Valentia province   53
Walk: Tropea   63
Catanzaro province   71
Cosenza province   77
Walk: Cosenza   83
Drive: Parco Nazionale della Sila 107
Crotone province   111
Walk: Crotone's *centro storico* 113

Features
The Society of Honourable Men   36
Tracing time   40
Cathedrals and churches   56
Calabrian arts and crafts   74
Calabrian cuisine: some like
    it hot!   88
The Grand Tour in Calabria   100
The Mezzogiorno   108
Aspects of archaeology   114
Language   154

Walks and tours
Walk: Reggio di Calabria   32
Drive: Parco Nazionale
    dell'Aspromonte   48
Walk: Tropea   62
Walk: Cosenza   82
Drive: Sila National Park   106
Walk: Crotone's *centro storico* 112

Introduction

Calabria is Italy's last frontier for tourism. While most of the country has been written about so much that no secrets are left, Calabria offers a wide range of experiences – from skiing through forests in winter, to hiking or horse riding as the snow abates, to diving through the crystal-clear waters of the Mediterranean – all with barely a tourist bus in sight. And, while you'll have to pinch yourself to realise you're still in Italy, once the food and wine arrive, there's no doubting where you are!

Italy is one of the most rewarding countries to visit. History, culture, food and wine, and a little romance, are the calling cards. Calabria offers this, but it rewards those who wish to get out of the comfort zone of the usual tourist trail. The most southern part of mainland Italy, Calabria forms the ankle to toe of the Italian 'boot', a rugged peninsula of legend since the time of Homer. The region has been, since then, an enviable prize for invaders and a safe haven for settlers, all of which adds to the fascinating mix of accents and architecture Calabria now possesses.

Calabria doesn't give up its secrets easily, though. While grapes, figs and olives grow in abundance, the dry heat of summer and the cold of winter have forced those who chose to settle here to be self-sufficient, practical and more than a little stubborn. Constant invaders have seen locals literally head for the hills to create new communities on precarious precipices, making

conquest difficult and life hard. The fact that Calabria has survived invasions, earthquakes and other disasters speaks volumes about the resilience of the people.

Today, after centuries of neglect by rulers and governments, Calabria is slowly asserting itself. The very things that ensured its survival – self-sufficiency, the remoteness of its many towns, and its ability to turn adversity into an asset – are what make it unique in Italy.

The 'new' Calabria celebrates its hearty and fiery cuisine, its handmade goods, and its stunning towns perched in improbable locations, boasting beautiful churches, castles and cobbled streets. The seaside towns offer splendid unspoilt beaches with azure waters, fresh seafood and laid-back charm, while twisting roads lead through pristine forest to the mountain towns, their picturesque scenery offering as equal a reward for your troubles as the charming villages that await your arrival. Activities such as horse riding, hiking or skiing in the crisp mountain air will help you work up an appetite for the hearty rustic cuisine of home-made sausage, freshly picked mushrooms, preserves of all persuasions, strong cheeses and robust wines.

While the locals know that they have something special, they've worked too hard for it to let it be taken for granted. Calabria may finally be ready to share, but it's not yet ready to compromise as some other Italian regions have.

Calabria is a unique, authentic part of Italy that surprises through the distinctive landscapes and endless coastlines, the resilient towns and equally hardy people that inhabit them, the hearty cuisine and the local customs. It is a region that the visitor needs to explore actively, but the rewards are great for those willing to take the time to discover the last frontier of a captivating country.

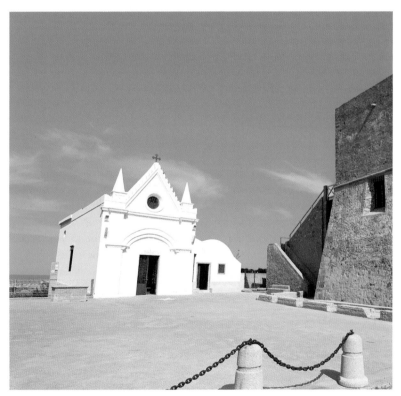

The Chiesetta della Madonna di Capo Colonna (1519) and a stone watchtower (1550) stand right next to the azure waters of the coast

Land and people

Italy consists of 20 regions, with Calabria part of the southern regions collectively known as the Mezzogiorno, or 'midday', because of the intensity of the sun there. The Mezzogiorno consists of Sicily, Sardinia and the regions of Abruzzi, Molise, Campania, Puglia, Basilicata and, of course, Calabria.

Calabria's population of just over 2 million is spread over the five provinces of the region: Catanzaro (CZ), Cosenza (CS), Crotone (KR), Reggio di Calabria (RC) and Vibo Valentia (VV). Catanzaro city, in the Catanzaro province, with a population of around 100,000, is the regional capital of Calabria.

The majority of Calabrians are Roman Catholic, but many also practise the Greek Orthodox faith. Patron saints abound, as do religious festivals to celebrate them. While the official language of Calabria is standard Italian, it's not always what you'll hear if you linger in the cafés or restaurants. Calabria has myriad dialects, often changing from village to village. The influences of the Greeks, French, Spanish, Albanians and Arabs (among many others!) see many Calabrian dialects having 'foreign' words mixed in. The more isolated the village, the more likely the dialect will be as strong as ever – and the less comprehensible it

will be to even other Calabrians, let alone Italians.

Geographically, Calabria is the instep and toe of the Italian 'boot', an irregularly shaped peninsula running northeast to southwest from the body of Italy, separating the Tyrrhenian and Ionian seas. At its base, the Strait of Messina separates it from Sicily, which, at its narrowest point between Punta Pezzo in Calabria and Capo Peloro in Sicily, is just over 3km (1¾ miles) wide.

While it may be something of a cliché to say this, Calabria really is a region of contrasts, with sub-zero temperatures in the mountains and extreme heat in summer in the valleys and on the beaches. And yes, you could, if you so wished, ski the slopes in the morning and take a dip in the crystal-clear Mediterranean waters in the afternoon.

Calabria's land area is just over 15,000sq km (5,800sq miles) and the peninsula is just 32km (20 miles) wide at its narrowest point, so nowhere in the region is more than 50km

A small lake in Sila National Park

(31 miles) from the 800km (500-mile) coastline. While it would appear that driving from coast to coast would be easy, over 90 per cent of Calabria's land surface lies 200m (660ft) above sea level, often rising dramatically from the sea itself. Three mountain ranges occupy the centre of the Calabrian land mass: from north to south, the Monte Pollino massif (highest point 2,267m/7,438ft), La Sila massif (1,928m/6,325ft) and the Aspromonte massif (1,956m/6,417ft).

The Pollino Mountains at their widest point form a natural barrier separating Calabria from the rest of Italy. The Pollino National Park, established in 1992, straddles Calabria and Basilicata and is the largest protected area in Italy. Within the park, there is a series of reserves as well as several peaks over 2,000m (6,560ft), with spectacular dolomitic limestone rock formations, waterfalls, gorges and rivers. The most

significant flora here, the Bosnian pine (*Pinus heldreichii*), is rare and this is one of the last remaining places it grows in Italy. The Italian wolf, eagles, falcons, vultures and the rare black woodpecker (*Dryocopus martius*) can also be spotted here.

La Sila consists of a massive plateau with an elevation of around 1,200m (3,940ft), with Botte Donato being the highest point at 1,928m (6,325ft). The area is a national park, Parco Nazionale della Sila, created in 2002 to replace the former National Park of Calabria. The park is home to some of Europe's most densely wooded areas, including Bosco di Fallistro, near the alpine village of Camigliatello, where giant trees hundreds of years old reside. It's famous for its sporting opportunities such as horse riding and cross-country skiing, as well as the wonderful mushrooms that people forage for. The opportunity to see wolves in their native environment attracts nature lovers as well.

The southernmost of the ranges is the Aspromonte massif, which is home to the Parco Nazionale dell'Aspromonte (the Aspromonte National Park). At the tip of the peninsula, this granitic-crystalline area is shaped like a pyramid and bordered on three sides by the sea. Species such as the wolf and owl are common, and rare species such as Bonelli's eagle are spotted here amid the pine, Sicilian fir, beech and chestnut trees that proliferate. Steep man-made terraces slope towards the sea from here, with grapevines, olive trees and citrus in evidence, including the bergamot, a rare citrus native to Calabria which is used to flavour Earl Grey tea (*see p143*). Visitors will be surprised to find prickly pear cactus as well.

The Ionian coast has long, flat, narrow beaches, while the Tyrrhenian coastline boasts white-sand beaches with spectacular settings such as those at the stunningly situated towns of Tropea and Scilla. Calabria offers a mix of white-sand and pebble beaches, all with crystal-clear waters that make diving a popular pastime. Sea life in the region is abundant, with swordfish, tuna, anchovies, sardines and mackerel sharing the waters with divers and swimmers.

Despite the rugged terrain of the area, Calabria has been prone to earthquakes of devastating magnitude. The last major destructive one was on 28 December 1908, centred on the Messina Strait and resulting in a large tsunami with a death toll of around 200,000. Other massive earthquakes in Calabria's history took place in 1693, 1783 and 1805.

Clean, clear water at Pizzo

History

3500 BC	The first villages are constructed and inhabitants begin agricultural work.
2000 BC	Enotrians (Arcadians), known for their love of wine, colonise Calabria.
1500 BC	Pre-Hellenic tribes such as the Laconians settle in the Calabrian region.
c. 750 BC	First Greek colonists appear in Reggio di Calabria and other areas, calling the region Magna Graecia ('Greater Greece').
400 BC	The Romans look to advance towards the south and start to wage war against their neighbours.
295 BC	The battle of Sentinum sees the Romans take control of central Italy.
203 BC	Hannibal, whose quest to defeat the Romans had all but failed and who had retreated to Calabria, is recalled to Carthage, leaving carnage in his wake.
AD 410	In his second invasion of Italy, Alaric the Visigoth sacks Rome, heads south, but contracts a fever and dies in Cosenza.
6th century	After a period of flux, the Byzantine era begins, flourishing in towns such as Stilo and Rossano.
902	The Saracens complete their conquest of Sicily and begin to attack Calabria.
1044	While the Saracens continue to attack Byzantine Calabria, the Normans begin their conquest of the region.
1130	Roger II is declared King of Sicily and all Norman-controlled areas in southern Italy, including Calabria.
1194	The Swabian (German) conquest of Calabria begins.
1266	Charles I of Anjou (France) becomes King of Sicily and rules Calabria.
1282	Charles is expelled from Sicily by the Sicilian Vespers and takes the mantle of King of Naples,

from where Calabria is then ruled.

1442	Alfonso V of Aragon becomes ruler of Naples and Sicily.
1494	Aragonese rule passes to the French, and the Italian Wars begin a year later.
1504–5	Squabbling over Naples and Sicily ends with the French, through the treaties of Blois, giving them to Spain.
1707	The cruel Spanish rule ends with the Austrian Habsburgs taking control.
1734	The Spanish Bourbons assume power.
1759–1806	Ferdinand IV of Naples rules with an iron fist.
1805–15	Relatives of Napoleon Bonaparte reign over the Kingdom of Naples.
1815	The Bourbons return.
1860	The unification of Italy occurs with Il Risorgimento ('The Resurgence').
1861	The Kingdom of Italy is proclaimed under King Vittorio Emanuele II.

1890	Mass emigration from the south begins.
1922	Benito Mussolini becomes prime minister.
1943	Italy surrenders to the Allies in World War II.
1945	Mussolini is captured and killed. World War II ends.
1946	Italians vote to abolish the monarchy.
1948	Italy becomes a parliamentary republic. Post-war emigration continues.
1950s– 1960s	Through the Cassa per il Mezzogiorno ('Fund for the South') the government tries to stimulate economic growth in the south.
1970s– 1980s	'Ndrangheta (Calabrian Mafia) gang wars begin.
2007–8	Gang tension leads to killings in Calabria and Germany and sweeping action by Calabrian police.
2010	Giuseppe Scopelliti, of Berlusconi's right-wing People of Freedom party, is victorious as regional president.

Politics

Italy is a parliamentary republic, with two legislative houses working under a constitution adopted in 1948 after the monarchy was abolished in 1946. It has a multi-party system, and executive power is exercised by a council of ministers led by a prime minister. Both houses of parliament as well as regional representatives elect a president for a seven-year term. The president is head of state and functions as a point of connection between the branches of power.

As for Italy's performance as a parliamentary republic, there are two sides to the coin. Italians greatly value their democratic rights – they just get to practise them rather too often! Since 1948 there have been 62 governments. Even since changes to the system, following the dawn of the 'Second Republic' in 1992, to combat political paralysis and corruption, political stability has not been forthcoming. For Italians, change is the only constant – apart from political stalwart Silvio Berlusconi's frequent appearances as prime minister (1994–5, 2001–6, 2008–).

At a 'state' level, Italy is divided into 20 regions (of which Calabria is one), whose governments have administrative powers, and these regions are further broken down into provinces and municipalities (*comuni*). Five of the regions have special autonomous capacity (Aosta Valley, Friuli-Venezia Giulia, Sardinia, Sicily and Trentino-Alto Adige), allowing them to enact legislation relating to local matters,

particularly to do with cultural minorities.

The southern regions, collectively known as the Mezzogiorno, consist of Abruzzi, Molise, Campania, Puglia, Basilicata, Sicily, Sardinia and Calabria. Calabria has five provinces: Catanzaro (CZ), Cosenza (CS), Crotone (KR), Reggio di Calabria (RC) and Vibo Valentia (VV). These provinces have their own elections, and a prefect is appointed to be the central government's representative in the region. Currently the Calabria region's governing party is the centre-left Partito Democratico (PD, Democratic Party).

The Presidente della Regione (regional president) is the head of the Giunta Regionale (regional government) and exercises executive power. He or she is elected for a five-year term. Legislative power lies with the Consiglio Regionale (regional council).

The constant changes in government at the national level are met with a shrug of the shoulders from locals in Calabria. Local issues are much more pertinent, although the same themes apply: corruption and incompetence of officials, as well as the feeling that those in the Mezzogiorno are treated as the poor cousins of the north. Nothing exemplifies this more than the long-promised bridge to Sicily from Calabria, which has been on and off the agenda for longer than anyone can remember. After being re-elected in 2008, Berlusconi put it back on the agenda and expects it to be completed by 2016, but most people in Calabria see the main benefit being to Sicily's Cosa Nostra and Calabria's 'Ndrangheta, who have an uncanny knack of being involved in any public works contracts in the region.

Public protests against the 'Ndrangheta increased in 2008 because of an incident in March when a child was shot in the head during a Mafia hit in Crotone, the third Mafia murder in a week in the region.

The Palazzo del Governo in Cosenza

Culture

When travellers think about Italian culture, what usually comes to mind first is the country's painting, sculpture, architecture, music, opera and literature, and then its traditional customs, folk arts and sport. While Calabria hasn't shared the long, continuous history of fine arts witnessed in other regions, it has boasted a small but accomplished body of painting and a rich architectural heritage, along with a vibrant popular culture, intriguing customs and fascinating folk traditions.

Mediterranean culture

In many respects, the Calabrians have more cultural connections to other Mediterranean peoples, such as the Greeks, Arabs, North Africans, Cypriots and Turkish, than they do to their northern Italian compatriots. Surrounded on three sides by the Mediterranean Sea and with a mountainous interior landscape that's home to remote hilltop villages, inevitably Calabria, like Sicily, has more in common with its rugged island neighbours than with Italy's northern land-bound regions.

The Greeks established colonies on the Ionian coast of Calabria in the 8th century BC that became the great Magna Graecia civilisation, and the remnants of their cultural influence are evident everywhere, but particularly in the language, customs and crafts, such as the techniques employed to produce village pottery and the designs and patterns that decorate ceramics, jewellery and textiles. The Arabs were also frequent visitors, leaving their mark on the cuisine, language and textiles, while the legacy of the Normans lies in the magnificent castle and church architecture. So it's natural that Calabrians share similar cultural traditions, customs and rituals revolving around village life, family and community, from the traditional male-dominated café on the main village piazza to the festivals focused around the rhythms of the seasons and celebrations of harvests.

Ironically, Calabria's isolation, underdevelopment, poverty, uneven distribution of wealth and the late arrival of a good road network, infrastructure and media have all contributed to helping preserve its wonderful rural traditions and folk culture.

Village life, folklore and customs

Calabria's hilltop towns and mountain villages may never be far from the coast, but they can seem worlds away in terms of their level of modernity and sophistication of everyday life and culture. Most of the Calabrians who remained in the small towns and villages after the mass emigrations to North America and Australia live a simple life on a low income by European standards. This is, after all, one of Italy's most underdeveloped regions.

In the most remote rural villages, many people are self-sufficient. Travel high in the mountains of the Aspromonte and around the Serra San Bruno and you'll see old men riding donkeys down the street, shepherds leading their flocks across hillsides, and old ladies in headscarves picking wild herbs that they collect in their long skirts. For those on holiday, the gentle pace of Calabria's rural life and the simple pleasures – the fresh air, idyllic countryside and rustic food – can be alluring.

What visitors to Calabria find particularly fascinating are the popular beliefs and superstitions that are alive here, many of which are also found throughout the villages of the Mediterranean and Arab world. For instance, some Calabrians believe in the *malocchio* ('evil eye'), a belief that envy or jealousy can cause something bad to happen and even bring about illness and, in the case of women, barrenness. They also believe that priests, hunchbacks and witches know how to cast the evil eye. Since ancient times it's been thought that witches are able to transform themselves into birds of prey and fly at night to steal babies. It's also believed that epilepsy is due to

Culture

Locals celebrate a football win in Amantea

Culture

supernatural causes and can be prevented if people carry pictures of a new moon.

Festivals

The Calabrians love a good festival, and they're a central feature of the culture of the region. Almost every week there's a religious, gastronomic, music, arts or folk festival on somewhere. Given the many historical influences, from ancient Greek and Roman to Byzantine and Norman, Calabria's religious festivals often combine Christian and pagan elements. Every town and village has a saint's day, where the priest leads processions carrying the statue of the Virgin through the streets.

Naturally, in a region that is agriculturally rich and where food is

such an important part of everyday life, gastronomic festivals (*sagre* in Italian) feature heavily on the calendar, with themed festivals held to celebrate the harvest of a certain crop or the slaughter of an animal. For instance, following the slaughter of pigs in January many towns celebrate *La Sagra de Maiale* ('Pork Feast'), where families prepare whole roasted pigs and other pork-based dishes that the village community enjoys together. You'll find every kind of food celebrated, from the mushroom to the potato, the swordfish to the strawberry!

Folk music

No other popular art form demonstrates Calabria's location at the crossroads of Mediterranean culture more than its folk music, which has been influenced by traditional songs from the Balkans, Eastern Europe, North Africa and the Levant. Calabria's underdevelopment, relative isolation and limited access to the media until recent decades has helped preserve its folk music traditions. The influence that is especially predominant is that of the Balkans in the music of northern Calabria's Albanian villages.

Many Calabrians still know and sing songs passed down from generation to generation, including lullabies sung to children, songs sung by farmers working the fields and harvesting their crops, and fishermen bringing in their catch, and songs for courting couples, weddings, religious processions and

Drummers in traditional costumes perform at the Festa della Bandiera in Morano Calabro

festivals. Instruments played include the lute, guitar, violin, *lira* (a type of fiddle), flute, accordion, bagpipes, harmonica and various percussion instruments.

The best recordings available are those by Calabrian ethnomusicologist Diego Carpitella, who documented folk songs from the region in the 1940s and 1950s. Now available through Columbia Music in the *Italian Treasury* series, their re-release in 2002 helped spark something of a folk music revival. It is nevertheless difficult to see live music performed, and your best hope is at a village festival.

The *passeggiata*

Everyone in Calabria religiously participates in the *passeggiata*, or collective evening stroll. The whole town dresses up – you can smell the shampoo, hairspray and perfume! – and strolls along the main pedestrian street, shopping thoroughfare or seaside promenade. It provides the opportunity to see and be seen, flirt, catch up with friends and family or buy a gelato. The best *passeggiata* is without a doubt in Vibo Valentia on a Sunday evening in summer, although the one in Reggio di Calabria is also well worth catching.

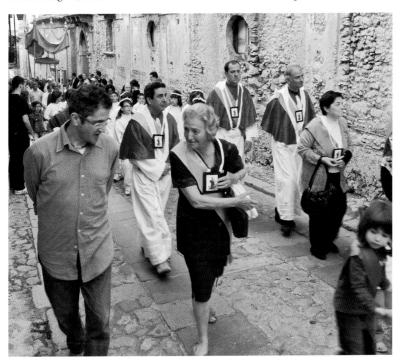

A religious procession wends its way through the streets of Gerace

Festivals and events

Calabria's calendar is crammed year-round with traditional festivals, religious processions and cultural events. While summer is the busiest time, it's also the best time for festivals, with the lidos of Reggio di Calabria and other seaside cities and towns lively with concerts and dance parties. Easter, village saint's days and seasonal harvests are also wonderful times to visit, when even the sleepiest villages come alive with street processions and community celebrations.

Dates can shift and events can be postponed from one year to the next, so check with the town's Pro Loco tourist office before planning a holiday around an event.

January
Il Concerto dell'Epifania (Epiphany Concert), Gerace
Sagra del Maiale (Festival of Pork), Bocchigliero

February
Sagra della Salsiccia e delle Polpette (Festival of Sausage and Baby Octopus), Acri

March
Fiera di San Giuseppe (Festival of St Joseph), Cosenza

April
L'Affruntata (religious procession of pagan origins held during Easter), Reggio di Calabria, Bagnara Calabra, Vibo Valentia

Pasqua procession (traditional Easter procession), Catanzaro, Gerace
Processione della Addolorata (Procession of the Golden Madonna), Nocera Tirinese
Sagra della Sguta (festival celebrating *sguta*, local sweet pastry), Siderno

May
Albanian Folklore Festival, San Basile, Tue after Pentecost
Festa della Bandiera (Festival of the Flag), Morano Calabro, end of May/early June
Madonna del Mare (Madonna of the Sea), Bova Marina
Reggio di Calabria Jazz Festival, Reggio di Calabria
Sagra delle Arance (Festival of Oranges), Trebisacce

June
Giro d'Italia (Italy's answer to the Tour de France), passes through Calabria

July

Altomonte Rock Festival, Altomonte

Festa della Madonna del Carmelo (Festival of the Madonna of Carmelo), Gerace

Festa del Sacro Cuore (featuring traditional dances), Gerace

Festival della Birra (Beer Festival), Marina di Gioiosa Jonica

Festival delle Invasioni (Festival of Invasions, music and culture festival), Cosenza

Madonna dell'Alto Mare Festival (Maritime Procession of the Madonna), Palmi, July or August

Maria SS delle Grazie Festival, Roccella Ionica

Outdoor Cinema Season, Anfiteatro alle Colonne, Roccella Ionica

August

Classical Theatre Season, Locri

Ethnic Music Festival, Locri

Festa dei Due Mari (Festival of the Two Seas), Altomonte

Festival Musicarchitettura (Arts Festival), Gerace

Festival del 'Nduja & 'Nduja Rock Festival (Festival of the Spicy Sausage Paste, followed by a Rock Music Festival), Spilinga

Mediterranean Summer Festival (concerts, theatre and film festival), Reggio di Calabria

National Puppet Theatre Festival, Roccella Jonica

Palio di Ribusa (medieval fair and tournament), Stilo

Pollino Music Festival (youth-oriented festival), San Severino Lucano

'Rumori Mediterrani' Roccella International Jazz Festival, Roccella Ionica

Sagra del Pesce Spada (Swordfish Festival), Bagnara Calabra

SilaInFesta, Festival di Musica Meticcia (Festival of Melting Pot Music), Camigliatello

Tropea Film Festival, Tropea

September

Calabria Festival, Villagio Mancuso

Diamante Madonna della Catena Festival (procession), Bruzzano Zeffirio

Festival Internazionale del Folklore (International Folklore Festival), Frascineto

Madonna della Consolazione (Lady of the City Festival), Reggio di Calabria

Palio di Diana (medieval festival), Vibo Valentia

October

Festa del Cioccolato (Chocolate Festival), Cosenza

Sagra dell'Uva e del Vino (Wine Festival), Donnici

San Arcangelo Crafts Fair, Delianuova Scillese Folklore Festival, Scilla

November

Sagra della Patata (Potato Festival), Camigliatello Silano

December

Presepi Viventi (Living Nativity Scene), Celico

Highlights

BASILICATA

Golfo di
Policastro

Golfo di
Taranto

Borgata Marina

Praia a Mare

Morano Calabro
6
Castrovillari
Parco Nazionale
del Pollino

Golfo di
Corigliano

Sibari

Altomonte **10**
Spezzano Albanese

COSENZA

Belvedere Marittimo

San Marco
Argentano
Rossano
Calopezzati

Cetraro

Punta Fiume Nicà

CALABRIA

Camigliatello Silano

Paola
O COSENZA 4
7
Cirò Marina

CROTONE

Parco Nazionale
della Sila
Cerenzia

Tyrrhenian
Sea

Lago **8**

Santa Severina

Amantea
Colosimi

CROTONE O
Capo
Colonna

Gimigliano
Petrona

Nicastro
Steccato

Tiriolo
Le Castella

Lamezia Terme International ✈
Capo
Rizzuto

CATANZARO
CATANZARO

Golfo di
Santa Eufemia

Golfo di
Squillace

Pizzo **2**
Squillace

Olivadi

VIBO VALENTIA

Tropea **1**
O

VIBO VALENTIA

Ionian
Sea

Capo Vaticano

Badolato Marina

Serra San Bruno

Nicotera
Stilo

Palmi

REGGIO DI
CALABRIA

SICILIA

3
Plati
Gerace
Siderno

Scilla
Parco Nazionale
dell'Aspromonte **5**

O Messina

9
O REGGIO DI CALABRIA

Stretto
di
Messina

✈
Aeroporto
dello Stretto

Bova Marina
Capo Spartivento

N

Page	
26–51	Reggio di Calabria
52–69	Vibo Valentia
70–75	Catanzaro
76–109	Cosenza
110–19	Crotone

1 Tropea With its pastel-coloured palazzi perched atop sheer chalky cliffs facing a crystal-clear aquamarine sea, Tropea is Calabria's most alluring city (*see pp58–63*).

2 Pizzo An elegant piazza lined with *gelaterie* sells Pizzo's famous tartufo ice cream in an enchanting old town (*see pp64–5*).

3 Scilla On one side of a castle-topped headland lies a white-sand beach backed by seafood tavernas; on the other are faded palazzi suspended over the sea (*see pp38–9*).

4 Camigliatello Silano A little mountain town, a gastronomic paradise and a centre for grand-touring, walking, horse riding, skiing and fishing (*see pp102–7*).

5 Aspromonte National Park It may be just a short drive from Reggio di Calabria, but this beautiful mountain region with its thick wooded forests seems worlds away (*see pp48–9*).

6 Morano Calabro The narrow alleyways of Calabria's most splendidly preserved medieval hill town are a delight to explore – competing only with the enchanting vistas of the town itself (*see p90*).

7 Calabrian wine The region's rich, spicy and rustic cuisine is well matched by its honest and robust wines, the best from Cirò Marina (*see p118*).

8 Amantea An elegant old town clings prettily to the mountain above a lively modern town, while the wide beach nearby buzzes in summer (*see pp84–5*).

9 Museo Nazionale The handsome Bronzi di Riace statues steal the show here, but Calabria's National Archaeological Museum has a wealth of other fascinating finds on display (*see p28 & pp29–30*).

10 Calabrian hill towns Ramshackle villages such as Altomonte and Belmonte sprawl charmingly across hilltops and tumble delightfully down mountains (*see p85 & pp90–91*).

Sunset at Tropea, with Santa Maria dell'Isola lit up

Suggested itineraries

Calabria boasts enough enchanting hilltop towns, splendid churches, scenic drives, pristine national parks and creamy beaches to occupy you for a month-long road trip. But if you want to take advantage of the cheap fares offered by low-cost airlines, Calabria also makes a wonderful weekend escape, with some of the region's best sights within a couple of hours' drive of its airports.

Long weekend

A perfect four-day weekend, starting from the airports of Reggio di Calabria or Lamezia Terme, should focus on Calabria's postcard-pretty towns of Tropea and Pizzo and the stunning scenery and surrounding beaches of the Violet Coast. Base yourself in either of the two towns and do a day trip to the other, visiting Vibo Valentia's historic centre and experiencing its lively *passeggiata* one evening. Spend a morning in Reggio di Calabria taking in the treasures of the Museo Nazionale and then drive up to the Aspromonte National Park for the afternoon to enjoy the fresh air and breathtaking landscapes.

One week

A week is not nearly long enough to undertake a food and wine tour of Calabria, but it will certainly give you a taste of the region's fiery cuisine and robust wines. Start with a night in Reggio di Calabria, dining at one of the city's excellent restaurants and trying the inventive gelato flavours from the *gelaterie* on Corso Garibaldi. The next day, drive up to Scilla for the night. At this town, renowned for its swordfish, you can watch the tall-masted boats bring the day's catch in, and then spend the afternoon feasting on fresh seafood at one of the many seaside trattorie. Continue north along the coast, spending a night at Tropea. Famous for its sweet red onions, Tropea is Calabria's dining capital, with scores of superb restaurants secreted away in its cobblestone lanes. Next stop should be a night each in Pizzo (for its celebrated chocolate tartufo ice cream), Amantea (for its marinated anchovies) and Camigliatello (for its gastronomic shops – buy some *peperoncini* – and dinner at one of Calabria's finest restaurants). With each meal, ask your waiter to recommend a local wine to wash it down with.

Alternatively, you could easily spend a week appreciating the art and architecture of Calabria's exquisite churches and cathedrals. At Reggio di Calabria, begin with the elegant cathedral, an imposing imitation of the original (built in 1453), which was destroyed in the 1908 earthquake, and Il Piccolo Museo San Paolo, home to an impressive collection of icons and religious relics. Aside from its other delights, Tropea requires a day to explore its stunning churches, particularly its Romanesque Norman cathedral. Further north, the town of Paola boasts several beautiful Baroque churches, although most pilgrims come for the Sanctuary of St Francis of Paola dating to 1435. Returning south, head inland for a scenic drive to La Certosa di Serra San Bruno, an extravagant Carthusian monastery, and to the east coast to Stilo to admire Calabria's most photographed church, the charming Byzantine-era Cattolica di Stilo. Further south, Gerace is legendary for once having 128 churches; its Norman cathedral is the largest in Calabria. You can drive south along the coast to Reggio di Calabria or north skirting the sea via Catanzaro to La Lamezia Terme; either way you'll pass a number of small towns boasting attractive squares dominated by lovely churches.

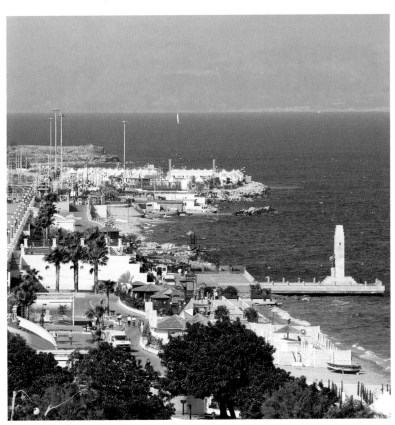

Reggio's waterfront looking over to Sicily

A figure at the church of Santa Maria della Consolazione in Altomonte

Two weeks

With two weeks, you can do a Grand Tour of Calabria, taking in all of the region's highlights. Beginning at Reggio di Calabria, spend a day each at Reggio, Scilla, Tropea, Pizzo and Vibo Valentia, before driving north. On the coast, elegant Amantea warrants an afternoon to appreciate its pretty old town, and inland the hilltop villages east of Amantea are worth a look on the scenic drive to Cosenza, whose labyrinthine old town is a delight to wander in. From here, drive north to the atmospheric mountain-top towns of Altomonte and Morano Calabro, both of which sprawl dramatically across their hills, providing spectacular sights in themselves while also offering up stunning vistas of the surrounding country. Returning south and inland to the Sila National Park, you can base yourself at alpine-like Camigliatello and spend a day exploring the area's alluring lakes and idyllic countryside. If you're here in winter, you can hit the slopes for a day's skiing, while the rest of the year you can walk, trek, fish and ride horses. Head east via the dramatically set San Giovanni in Fiore and Santa Severina to the seaside town of Crotone, which boasts a lively beachfront promenade and an attractive centre with elegant shopping arcades. On your way south, call in to see the extraordinary sight of Le Castella, a Norman castle that, from the right vantage point, appears to float at sea. It's an easy run along the flat coastal plain (although in summer the going can be slow), so stop at Squillace for a quick visit to admire its attractive square on your way to Stilo, where you should stay the night. Visit Stilo's bewitching Byzantine cathedral in the morning when the light's at the best angle. Take the picturesque road inland under the leafy canopies of trees to the Serra San Bruno and its magical monastery before returning to the west coast.

Longer

One month means you can slow your pace down to something more closely resembling the Italian way of life. Stick to the two-week itinerary above, but spend longer at places such as Scilla and Tropea so you can schedule in some beach time for swimming, sunbathing and watersports, and perhaps a cruise to the Aeoli Islands and Stromboli. Extend your stay at Camigliatello and the Sila National Park to a few days to allow for some leisurely walking, fishing or horse riding. Add a couple of days at the Pollino National Park in the far north, where you should also visit the fascinating Albanian-speaking villages of Frascineto and Civita. From there drive to Sibari to see the excellent archaeological museum with finds from the nearby ruins, and Rossano to get a glimpse of the purple codex, take in the impressive cathedral and elegant city buildings, and tour the delightful Amarelli liquorice factory and museum. On the southeast coast add a night at Gerace and a day or two to drive or trek the Aspromonte National Park.

Suggested itineraries

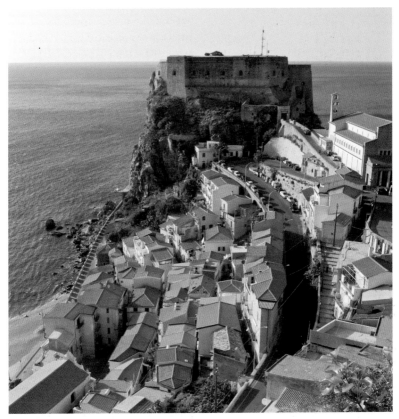

The old town of Scilla, one of the most scenic towns on the coast

Reggio di Calabria province

Seductively surrounded by a sparkling cobalt sea on three sides and bordering the provinces of Vibo Valentia and Catanzaro in the north, the Reggio di Calabria province forms the toes of Italy's pointy boot. Rather aptly, the more alluring cities of Reggio di Calabria, Scilla, Bagnara Calabra and Palmi are on the west coast, wriggling their pretty painted nails, while the slightly shabby and rather charmless towns of Bovalino, Locri and Siderno are on the east coast, the underside and ball of Italy's boot.

Even more appropriately, hidden away in the interior are the mysterious and mesmerising medieval hilltop towns of Gerace and Stilo and, in the impenetrable Aspromonte Mountains, the remote ramshackle villages of Roghudi, Roccaforte del Greco, Casalnuovo and San Stefano in Aspromonte, in an area commonly known as the cradle of Calabria's Mafia, the 'Ndrangheta.

Reggio is blessed with some of the most beautiful landscapes of Calabria, from the dramatic coastline of the province's western shore where enormous emerald mountains majestically meet the Tyrrhenian Sea, suddenly dropping away to sheer cliffs and rocky headlands hiding jagged bays and sandy beaches, to the steep mountains of the isolated interior with meadows blanketed by wild flowers, tall, dark forests, and deep, hidden valleys carved by dry, rocky river beds.

Wherever you go, the provincial capital aside, the air is startlingly fresh and aromatic, either smelling of the sea or fragrant with the honey-scented yellow broom flower, a constant presence in the countryside. Known as the *plante de genêt*, a sprig of it was worn in battle by Geoffrey V, Count of Anjou, of the Angevin dynasty that dominated Calabria for so long.

The birthplace of Gianni Versace, Bagnara Calabra is a pleasant seaside town

Reggio di Calabria province

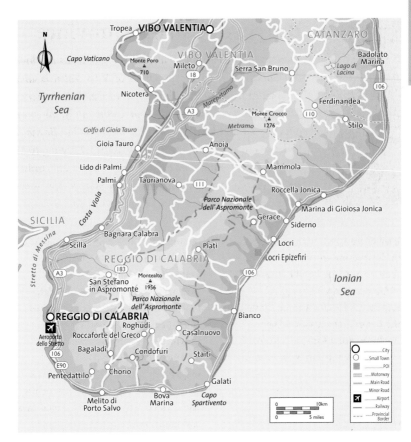

The region is one of delightful extremes. In the cities and large towns well-dressed locals, young and old, participate in the afternoon *passeggiata*, sauntering arm in arm, eating gelati and admiring the latest fashions in the chic shop windows, while in the ancient rural interior headscarved old ladies scoop up wild herbs gathered from the hillside in their long skirts, and shepherds in braces and breeches follow their flocks down lonely dirt tracks.

CALABRIA: A REAL ESTATE HOTSPOT?

Many investors see Calabria as the last great real estate bargain in the Mediterranean – and it probably is, despite prices having risen by 30 per cent between 2008 and 2010. Previously, investments were made largely by Italians themselves, many of them northerners looking for sunny southern holiday homes. But the government's big push in tourism to the region has started to entice people from other EU countries, particularly Germans, Dutch and Brits. Predictions are that prices may rise a further 15 per cent over the next few years.

Reggio di Calabria

Founded in the 8th century BC by Greek colonisers on the advice of the Oracle of Delphi, the *polis* of Rhegion was to become one of the great cities of Magna Graecia. It was strategically situated for military domination, with its excellent position on the Tyrrhenian and Ionian seas, and was primed for cultural and economic growth, located as it was on established Mediterranean trade routes.

Aligning with Rome during the 3rd century BC, Rhegion gradually adopted the customs and lifestyle of the Romans, while still maintaining the Greek language. Attacked by Hannibal and the Carthaginians in 211 BC, it was defended by the Romans, thus becoming a federate state, and in 89 BC was renamed Rhegium Julium. During this period a forum was established where Piazza Italia now lies, and the city was enriched with splendid architecture, grand villas and palaces, and eight thermal baths.

After being invaded by Barbarians, though, the city began a slow decline, compounded by subsequent invasions by Arabs, Byzantines and then Normans in 1060. Thereafter it was dominated by Swabians, Angevins, Aragonese, Spanish and Saracens, and it wasn't until the 17th century that the city was returned to its earlier splendour. Elegant buildings such as the Palazzo del Governo were constructed, and the Duomo was restored, only for it to suffer once again under Bourbon domination and then from natural catastrophe with the 1783 earthquake.

In 1860, Garibaldi and his troops freed Reggio from the Bourbons, and the city was finally rebuilt; along with the Unity of Italy, Reggio was reborn. Unfortunately, the new mood didn't last long, and in 1908 Reggio was struck by another earthquake and a tsunami. The loss of life and structural damage were devastating. The Fascist period resulted in some expansion and modernisation of the city, but Reggio essentially remained underdeveloped and depressed, and in 1970 lost its role as regional capital to Catanzaro.

Today, though, as the provincial capital, Reggio is Calabria's most densely populated urban centre, yet, aside from the busy port and clogged traffic on the motorways, it doesn't feel like a big city. Its gorgeous location on the sea, endless sunny skies, and the

THE MYSTERY OF THE MISSING BRONZE

The two Bronzi di Riace (Riace bronzes) are the pride of Reggio di Calabria and one of the most important archaeological finds of the 20th century, but were there more than two bronzes lying on the seabed when the statues were found? Reports of what was discovered by a Roman chemist, Stefano Mariottini, on holiday in 1972 still conflict with what is currently on display in the Museo Nazionale della Magna Grecia. Mariottini's claim to this day that he saw a 'group' of statues still raises concern that at least one bronze went missing before the official dives began to recover them, and it's still a hot topic of conversation in Calabria.

palm trees along the attractive Lungomare (waterfront) give Reggio a summer-holiday feel throughout the year. Yet the city's elegant architecture, fine museums, and excellent restaurants and cafés all combine to lend Reggio a level of sophistication other cities in Calabria just don't have.

Museo Nazionale di Reggio Calabria (National Museum of Reggio Calabria)
This is Reggio's, if not Calabria's, main attraction and is indeed unmissable. The outstanding museum houses a vast collection including a wealth of precious finds from the Magna Graecia period, the highlights of which are the world-famous 2m (6½ft) high bronze statues of Riace, dating from around 450 BC. These tall, handsome male nudes were found on the bottom of the sea (*see box*), most likely thrown overboard when the ship carrying them encountered difficulty. Apart from their size, what makes them so impressive is their exquisite shape and form – the ripples in their muscles and the inclination of a hip – and the intricacy of details such as their hair. Another bronze known as the Philosopher's Head is also superb.

The museum comprises three floors. Prehistoric exhibits and the Locri collection are on the ground floor, displays of finds from Rhegion, Metaurus, Medma, Kaulon and Krimisa are on the first, while the underwater archaeology collection is (fittingly) displayed in the basement.

The finds here from the 95ha (235-acre) Locri Epizefiri site are far more impressive than those at Locri itself. There's an abundance of fascinating items on display, including delicate jewellery, ornaments and miniature mirrors (something Locri was famous for producing), alabaster ointment boxes and strigils (curved blades) used by athletes to scrape the oil from their bodies after exercising, and tiny toys, such as terracotta dolls and a bronze chariot.

Terracotta votive plaques testify to the importance of the goddess

The Museo Nazionale holds the greatest treasures of the Calabrian region

Persephone at Locri. The hall of archives from the temple of Zeus, dating from the 4th to 3rd centuries BC, consists of 39 inscribed bronze tablets that record loans the temple made to the city. The marble Dioscuri sculptures from Paros are significant.

What is most extraordinary about the finds from Rhegion is that everything on display was found by chance from excavations in the city not undertaken for archaeological reasons. Imagine what they'd find if they actually looked! One particularly fascinating display contains 6th-century BC painted cups, bowls, statuettes and votive plaques, while another contains a famous 3rd-century glass cup decorated with hunting scenes and gold leaf. *Piazza de Nava. Tel: (0965) 812 255. www.museonazionalerc.it. At the time of writing closed for renovation with a projected opening date of March 2011.*

Il Piccolo Museo San Paolo (Little Museum of St Paul)

This is a hidden gem, secreted away down a lane behind the lovely **Chiesa di San Paolo** (Church of St Paul), itself decorated with jaw-dropping gold mosaics. The tiny museum is home to a magnificent private collection of sacred icons and beautiful paintings, brought together by parish priest Monsignor Francesco Gangemi, who has been collecting since the 1930s. Easily deserving exhibition rooms as grand as those of the Pinacoteca (*see below*), the important collection is currently

arranged rather haphazardly in two dusty rooms and a basement at the back of the church.

Highlights include paintings and sketches by Antonello de Messina, Raphael, Giovanni Bellini and Vincenzo da Pavia, as well as other significant southern Italian and European artists. Most impressive is the collection of some 170 Russian icons dating from the 15th to 19th centuries, as well as fine liturgical silverware, ivory objects and brocade paraments. A visit here can easily be added to the town walk (*see pp32–3*).
Via Reggio Campi, Vico Sorgona 4/c. Tel: (0965) 892 426. Open: Wed & Sat–Sun 9am–noon, other times by appointment. Donations welcome.

La Pinacoteca Civica (Municipal Art Gallery)

This *pinacoteca* or 'picture gallery' is one of Reggio's delights. Housed in the Museo Nazionale until it moved to swish new premises in 2008, in the same building as the Teatro Comunale Francesco Cilea (Francesco Cilea Municipal Theatre), this small but splendid collection was donated by some of the city's most illustrious families. The paintings are beautifully presented against bold walls in sumptuous high-ceilinged rooms illuminated by chandeliers, and the exhibition is compact in size, so it won't take you more than an hour to enjoy some wonderful works by some of the region's finest artists.

Calabrian artists may not be as widely known as those from other regions of Italy, yet Calabria has produced a number of great painters who are exhibited here. Mattia Preti (1613–99), known as the Cavaliere Calabrese ('Calabrian Knight'), is probably the region's most renowned artist. The theme of repentance and forgiveness as exemplified in *Return of the Prodigal Son* (1670) features in a lot of his paintings. Vincenzo Cannizzaro (1740–68) was born in Reggio di Calabria and studied in Naples under Francesco de Mura. He painted rural landscapes, castles, hunting scenes and portraits. His *Fall of the Magus* is impressive.

Look out also for work by 19th-century painters Giuseppe Benassai (1835–78) and Demetrio Salazar (1822–82) from Reggio di Calabria, and Andrea Cefaly (1827–1907) from Catanzaro. Benassai studied in Naples and Florence, showed his work in Paris and travelled to Egypt. His *The Calm* (1868) and *Aspromonte* (1869) accurately depict the idyllic, rugged Calabrian countryside. Salazar mainly painted portraits, while Cefaly was known for his battle scenes, including the splendid *Battle of Capua* (1860), commissioned by Vittorio Emanuele II. *Piazza Italia 1. Tel: (0965) 324 822. Open: Tue–Sun 10am–12.30pm & 4.30–7.30pm. Admission charge.*

La Pinacoteca Civica is Reggio di Calabria's elegant new art gallery

Walk: Reggio di Calabria

This relaxed walk around Reggio di Calabria takes in the best sights, museums and churches of the city. It's best attempted in the cool of the late afternoon or early evening after the shops have reopened and the locals have freshened up and ventured out for their passeggiata, *the ritual see-and-be-seen promenade along Corso Giuseppe Garibaldi.*

Allow two hours for the walk.

The walk begins and ends at Reggio's superb Museo Nazionale di Reggio Calabria, so you could visit the museum before your saunter.

1 Museo Nazionale di Reggio Calabria (National Museum of Reggio Calabria)

After admiring the handsome Riace bronze statues at the superb National Museum (*see pp29–30*), cross the road to Piazza de Nava to take in the museum's imposing Fascist architecture. The square is dedicated to statesman Giuseppe de Nava, depicted in the centrepiece marble statue by sculptor Francesco Jerace.

Cross Via Vollaro, turn right and walk one block in the direction of the sea to Piazza Indipendenza, then cross the road again to 'Cesare'.

2 Gelateria Cesare

This dark-green kiosk is the city's most popular *gelateria*. Join the queue – it's worth the wait!

Cross Viale Matteotti, walk one block up to Largo Colombo and turn right on to Corso Giuseppe Garibaldi.

3 Corso Giuseppe Garibaldi

Stroll along Reggio's main pedestrian-only shopping street, admiring the elegant architecture and stylish fashion in the boutique windows. Rebuilt after the devastating earthquake and tsunami of December 1908, many of the buildings are neoclassical or Art Nouveau.
Continue along Corso Giuseppe Garibaldi until you reach the grand Teatro Comunale Francesco Cilea on your left.

4 Teatro Comunale Francesco Cilea and La Pinacoteca Civica

Head up the stairs, through the glass doors and slide across the polished marble floors to get a look inside this sumptuous theatre, with its red velvet curtains and intricately decorated ceiling, that has played host to the great Maria Callas. Although completed in

1930, it's in a style typical of 19th-century theatres. If it's closed, check out later performance times to return for, then call in to the Pinacoteca Civica, Reggio's finest art museum (*see pp30–31*), before grabbing a coffee at B'Art Café, both in the one building. *Cross the road to visit Piazza Italia.*

5 Piazza Italia

Marking the centre of the city, this leafy square is named after the lovely *Monumento all'Italia* statue dedicated to the Martyrs of the Revolt of 1847. The creamy statue of a beautiful crowned woman in robes looks particularly striking against the elegant Palazzo del Governo building in the

background. As you leave the square, look to your right down towards the sea for the stunning *Il Monumento ai Caduti* topped with its winged victory bronze.
Continue along Corso Giuseppe Garibaldi for two blocks, turning left into Via Ottimati to Piazza Castello.

6 Castello Aragonese (Aragonese Castle)

Built by the Angevins on Norman foundations, strengthened by Ferdinand I of Aragon in 1458, and extended by the Viceroy of Naples, Pedro of Toledo, from 1532 to 1553, the castle was damaged by the 1783 and 1908 earthquakes, was partly demolished (losing two towers) to

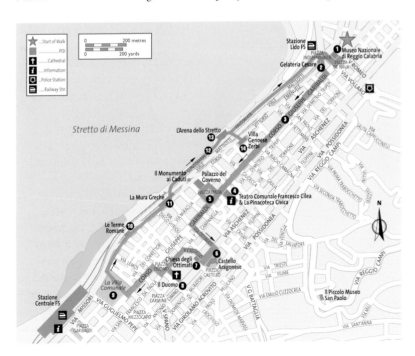

facilitate better traffic movement, and partly collapsed during reinforcement in 1986. The surviving sections house temporary art exhibitions.

Cross Via Castello and visit Chiesa degli Ottimati.

7 Chiesa degli Ottimati (Church of the Optimates)

A Byzantine church once stood here but fell victim, like so many other city buildings, to one catastrophe after another and was demolished following the 1908 earthquake. This building, constructed in 1931 and dedicated to Santa Maria Annunziata, features Byzantine, Arab and Norman influences. The striking black-and-white floor mosaics are Roman in design. The beautiful painting on the main altar, *L'Annunciazione* (1597), is by Florentine artist Agostino Ciampelli.

A statue outside the Duomo

Walk down Via Castello, turn left and walk along Via Tommaso Campanella to the cathedral.

8 Il Duomo (Cathedral)

Churches have stood here since 1453, yet all were destroyed by raids or earthquakes. This opulent cathedral in an eclectic Romanesque and Gothic style was rebuilt after the last earthquake of 1908 and reconsecrated in 1928. The elegant façade boasts a beautiful rose window with floral cornice, and either side of the entrance stairs are statues of San Paolo (St Paul) and Santo Stefano da Nicea (St Stephen of Nicea), Reggio's first bishop. The engraved bronze portals are impressive in their detail. Inside you'll find beautiful Baroque marble altars and tombs, splendid paintings and a prettily decorated ceiling.

Cross Piazza Duomo and continue along Corso Giuseppe Garibaldi until you arrive at the public gardens.

9 La Villa Comunale (Public Gardens)

Exotic plants from Asia and Australia flourish alongside Mediterranean foliage in these leafy public gardens, established in 1896. A pretty 19th-century portal stands on one of the avenues, one of the few survivors of the 1908 earthquake. Impressive bronze, marble and stone busts and statues decorate the park.

Exit on to Corso Vittorio Emanuele/Viale Matteotti, then cross the road to the garden in the centre of the boulevard.

10 Le Terme Romane (Roman Baths)

Dating from when Rhegium Julium was a prosperous city of the Roman Empire, this Roman thermal bath complex, discovered in 1883, is the only one preserved of the eight found in the city.
Continue until you reach La Mura Greche.

11 La Mura Greche (Greek Wall)

Two parallel rows of travertine stone blocks are all that is left of the 4th-century BC defensive walls of the Greek *polis*, Rhegion.
Cross the road again to the Lungomare Falcomatà.

Late afternoon stroll along the Lungomare (waterfront)

12 Lungomare Falcomatà

Reggio's stunning seafront boasts two walkways, an upper promenade running beside Corso Vittorio Emanuele/Viale Matteotti and a lower pathway running along the seaside, the Lungomare Falcomatà. In the late afternoon, locals walk, jog, rollerblade, cycle, push chairs and eat gelati here, admiring the views of Sicily and Mount Etna. In summer, lidos are set up along the Lungomare and the city's nightlife relocates itself to here, with beach bars and clubs opening until late.
Stroll along the waterfront and stop at the arena.

13 L'Arena dello Stretto

This cream marble memorial marks the spot where Vittorio Emanuele III landed as a sovereign on national soil for the first time on 31 July 1900. The beautiful bronze statue *Athena Promachos* (*Athena who Fights in the Front Line*) is by Sicilian sculptor Bonfiglio.
Walk up the steps beside the arena to Corso Vittorio Emanuele and cross the road.

14 Villa Genoese Zerbi

This gorgeous red-brick villa, built in 1925 by architect-engineers Zerbi, Pertini and Magrats, was modelled on a typical 14th-century Venetian palace. Note the Gothic-style arches and decorative capitals on the columns, each slightly different in design. The villa hosts brilliant exhibitions of contemporary art.
Cross the road to the Lungomare and continue strolling. When you reach Piazza Indipendenza, it might be time for another gelato.

The Society of Honourable Men

When people think of the Mafia, perhaps the caricatures of the *Godfather* films – or the Cosa Nostra (Sicilian Mafia), which inspired the novels and these films – come to mind, but the reality is that the lesser-known Calabrian Mafia, the 'Ndrangheta, is now far more powerful and just as ruthless.

The 'Ndrangheta was traditionally a low-key operation, and it was the hail of bullets that killed six men from San Luca (eastern Reggio di Calabria) in a payback hit in the German city of Duisburg in 2007 that made the authorities take notice of how cold-blooded the organisation had become.

In mid-2008 the Australian police took credit for the world's biggest bust of the drug Ecstasy (4.4 tonnes) – disguised as tins of tomatoes. It was later revealed that the tomatoes, and another shipping container discovered a month earlier carrying 150kg (330lb) of cocaine, were attributed (along with money-laundering activities) to the Australian arm of the 'Ndrangheta. There was no escaping the fact that the Calabrian Mafia had become big players in the world's illegal drug trade.

The 'Ndrangheta – the name derives from the Greek word for a noble man – is known as the 'Society of Honourable Men'. The original Mafia, born in Sicily, arose out of small private armies that challenged rulers who were hard on the local population. Their code of *omertà* means never to cooperate with the authorities, even when a crime has been committed against you.

This code was also adopted by the 'Ndrangheta, who gathered strength in the years after World War II. Unlike the rigid pyramid structure of the Cosa Nostra, the 'Ndrangheta has a fairly horizontal structure, where nobody really knows the level of another member, or, if they do, it's information never shared. Because of the family nature of the organisation – there are apparently around 150 families involved – it is uncommon for a member to cooperate with the authorities.

In the past the 'Ndrangheta operated only in Calabria, and their activities focused on extortion and blackmail. John Paul Getty III, held captive for around six months during which one of his ears was posted to his family, was their most high-profile victim. However, a series of gang wars erupted in the 1970s and 1980s, and by the 1990s the 'Ndrangheta had begun expanding operations, both to northern Italy and to the rest of the world. They formed ties to Colombian drug cartels and took control of drug trafficking across Europe, and they now have an estimated US$50 billion in business assets.

One of the factors that enabled their successful expansion was migration to other countries where family members set up satellite branches of the 'Ndrangheta. Besides Colombia, countries such as Australia, Canada and Germany are just some of those with strong 'Ndrangheta ties. However, no matter how far they go or how powerful they have become, the 'Ndrangheta always sees Calabria as its home.

The head of the 'Ndrangheta, Pasquale Condello, who had been on the run for 20 years, was finally captured in early 2008 in Reggio di Calabria. While some members sport fancy houses and a lavish lifestyle, many live modestly in their villages.

Calabrians who are not part of the 'Ndrangheta dislike the fraternity but acknowledge that, if they want to start a business in Calabria, they'll probably have to deal with the 'Ndrangheta at some stage because of its expansion into legitimate areas of activity. But it's not something that's explicit: it's simply implied that you're dealing with a 'family'.

The area around Locri is known as a hotbed of 'Ndrangheta activity

The west coast: La Costa Viola (Violet Coast)

Gioia Tauro

This former Magna Graecia city is now a rather scruffy modern town of dilapidated buildings and half-completed grey concrete blocks. There is a lovely long, wide, creamy beach, but it's backed by some dodgy bars. In the compact older part of town there are several beautiful Baroque buildings and a few churches worthy of a quick look. The port is Italy's biggest and the second largest on the Mediterranean, but, according to a 2008 Italian parliamentary commission report, it's controlled by the 'Ndrangheta, the Calabrian Mafia, which uses the facility for illegal trafficking.

Palmi

The so-called 'jewel of the Costa Viola' according to the tourism marketing brochures, Palmi was popular with the English aristocracy at the turn of the last century but is now a shabby town, and its seaside quarter, Lido di Palmi, is not much better. The beach itself is beautiful and there are spectacular views down the coastline to the south, but it is accessible only by boat. The steep terraced slopes between the town and beach are lovely, covered with groves of oversized olive trees and gravity-defying grapevines that are definitely worth a look but don't warrant an overnight stay.

Scilla

Sprawled over a rocky headland that juts into the aquamarine sea, Scilla is one of Calabria's most alluring towns. On one side of the headland – crowned with an imposing castle – is a long, wide, white-sand beach backed by colourful houses stacked up high to the top of the hill. On the other side of the bluff is the charming old neighbourhood of Chianalea, with its pretty pastel-painted houses squeezed between sea and road. As it sits right beside the water, waves can crash dramatically against the buildings, but on a calm day there could be no lovelier place to be with a glass of wine than on the wooden deck of a restaurant overlooking the sea.

There is very little to do at Scilla, other than visit **Castello Ruffo** (Ruffo Castle) and explore the atmospheric streets of the upper town and its few

---

BAGNARA CALABRA'S BELOVED SON

Being the birthplace of Calabria's most famous son on the world stage, the fashion designer Gianni Versace (born 1946), it's rather apt that Bagnara Calabra, a seaside town halfway between Scilla and Palmi, should have an atmosphere of decayed elegance about it. Versace's mother was a dressmaker and he worked for her as an apprentice. He then studied architecture before moving to the home of Italian fashion, Milan, opening his first boutique in 1978 after creating successful collections for other designers. His career took off and Versace became the name and face of one of the most recognisable fashion houses in the world. He died at the hands of a serial killer in his adopted home of Miami in 1997.

churches, but that's just the way its devoted fans like it. Action centres on the beach and lidos by day. In the afternoons, a stroll to the fishing harbour is warranted to watch the daily catch of swordfish come in. And, in the evenings, a feast of fresh seafood at one of the waterfront restaurants is best followed by a moonlit walk along the shore. Scilla is incredibly popular in summer and on weekends throughout the year, when it's advisable to book ahead.

Balconied waterfront buildings at Scilla

Tracing time

Calabria is one of the few parts of Italy with a significant non-Italian minority. The Albanians, for instance, settled in Calabria in the 15th and 16th centuries after fleeing the Turks who had invaded their homeland, and have retained their religion and language to this day in their northern Calabrian villages. But what have others who have come to Calabria, including the many invaders, left behind? And how has this contributed to the Calabria that we know today?

Some of the first settlers in Calabria were Oscan-speaking tribes around the Iron Age (11th century BC). One of the tribes was the Oenotri, the vine cultivators, and, indeed, the southern region of Italy has long been known as 'the land of the grape'. Then there were the Itali, who may have given the country the name 'Italy'.

The Greeks settled in the southern and eastern parts of Calabria bordering the Ionian Sea around 750 BC, giving the area the name Magna Graecia, or Greater Greece. During this period wine cultivation flourished. As a result, Calabria's two main grape varieties are of Greek origin. Other forms of Greek culture were exported to the region as well, including a variety of the Greek alphabet, the Cumae, which the Latins adopted and which evolved into what is the most common alphabet used today. A dialect of the Greek language is still spoken in some parts of Calabria.

Magna Graecia was absorbed into the Roman realm after the Pyrrhic War (280–275 BC), and after the fall of Rome the area came under the domination of the Byzantine Empire. While Byzantine Calabria was absorbing eastern influences into all spheres of life, churches and monasteries were built in a Greek tradition, such as La Cattolica in Stilo and San Marco Evangelista in Rossano.

The Arabs and Germanic Lombards also had influence. The Arab, or Saracen, impact can be seen today in the cuisine, especially the use of spices such as cloves and nutmeg, hot peppers and the ubiquitous aubergine. While the Arabs never gained a strong foothold, the trade that their presence generated helped infuse these influences into Calabrian life.

The Norman conquests (1054–1194), from which the remains of castles and towers still exist

Le Castella: a splendid Norman castle that appears to float at sea

throughout the region, also left their mark with the introduction of a feudal system that lasted beyond the unification of the nation in 1860.

The Swabian (German), Angevin (French) and Aragonese (Spanish) eras were followed by another 200 years of Spanish rule from the early 1500s. What is interesting about this period is the number of Jewish people living in Calabria. Evidence of their settlement dates from the 4th century in Reggio, and it's believed that a reasonable proportion of the Calabrian population was Jewish and had been forced to convert before the time of the Inquisition. Many say that Calabrian cuisine is also influenced by Jewish food, while they also had an impact on silk and leather production.

The Bourbons followed the Spanish, and their unforgiving rule led to Calabrian insurrections and the formation of secret societies – the precursor to the modern-day Mafia.

Reggio di Calabria province

If you head to the pretty fishing town of Scilla and are thinking of taking a dip, look out for Scylla, a beast with twelve feet, six necks with awful heads attached and mouths full of black death. Such were the findings of Homer in *The Odyssey*. The poet Virgil, who modelled some of his works on Homer's, caught a fever in Calabria and died; his epitaph (apparently self-penned) states *Calabri rapuere* or 'Calabria snatched me away'. Myths and legends abound in Calabria even today – just ask about the Mafia or the third Riace Bronze!

The south and east coasts

Aside from the splendid Parco Nazionale dell'Aspromonte (Aspromonte National Park), the southern part of the Reggio di Calabria province has few sights of interest to travellers. Immediately south of the city of Reggio di Calabria, a string of pleasant beaches provides weekend escapes for Reggio's residents, and windsurfing is particularly popular here. However, foreign visitors are likely to be more interested in diversions inland in the Aspromonte mountains and in villages such as Pentedattilo and Roghudi.

Chorio

Sprawled picturesquely over a bend in the dry River Tuccio in the lower Aspromonte, Chorio is the birthplace of Padre Gaetano Catanoso. Born here in 1879, the priest was canonised in 2005 for two healing miracles attributed to him and a lifetime of service to Reggio di Calabria's poor. Padre Catanoso used

to hike or ride a donkey to the surrounding mountain villages to bring hope, faith and help to the destitute. He founded an order of nuns from the area's poverty-stricken families, and they worked hard to help him assist their people by establishing schools and homes for the elderly in villages such as Chorio, San Lorenzo and Roccaforte del Greco. Both Chorio and the saint have received quite a bit of attention since the release in June 2008 of the book *My Cousin the Saint* by his American relative, journalist Justin Catanoso. There is a statue of the saint in the piazza at Chorio and a plaque at Pentedattilo.

Pentedattilo

Named Pentedattilo from the Greek word *pentedaktylos* (meaning 'five fingers'), this atmospheric village is breathtakingly situated at the base of a striking rock formation that looks like an enormous hand raised to the sky. As you approach the abandoned village, you'll need some moments to make out the crumbling buildings, as their sandstone bricks blend seamlessly with the rocky peaks behind and the boulders that appear to tumble down the mountainside.

Once comprehended, it's an incredibly dramatic sight that makes for a memorable first impression. You will want to stop to absorb the scene and take some photographs at the bend before the entrance to the hamlet. In winter or after rain, the green grass and lush vegetation on the slopes below the village create an especially splendid scene. It's even more captivating in early spring, when wild flowers explode with colour on the hills, which are normally barren throughout the summer and autumn months.

While the location of Pentedattilo – at the foothills of the Aspromonte and with panoramic views to the Ionian Sea – is unbeatable, the village itself is a ghost town. It was semi-abandoned after the 1783 earthquake severely damaged its buildings (only its Greek residents remained), and then deserted completely after landslides following the earthquake of 1908, which left all of its buildings virtually uninhabitable.

The origins of the village are much debated, with some scholars claiming it to be Byzantine or even Greek in origin, its birth dating back as far as 700 BC, while others argue that the site was chosen as a Roman military garrison because of its excellent defensive position.

What is certain is that Pentedattilo enjoyed its greatest period of splendour in the 14th century as a seat of nobles before entering a period of decline after the ruling Alberti family of Messina was massacred at Easter 1686 by Bernardino, the son of Pentedattilo's former landlord, the Baron of Montebello. While the families had feuded for some time over territorial claims, the story goes that the son and his men murdered the Albertis in their beds after Marquis Alberti refused Bernardino permission to marry his daughter Antonietta.

The result was a bloodbath, and, when the wind howls through the surrounding valley, the locals believe it's the marquis crying out in anger at the loss of his family and land. A stroll through the ghost town of roofless

Reggio di Calabria province

Pentedattilo's old town is considered a 'ghost town'

View along the coast towards Bova Marina

the right after Chorio and a few kilometres before Bagaladi.

Bagaladi

Another atmospheric lower Aspromonte town, Bagaladi is thought to take its name from descendants of the Arab Bahalà family to which a Norman noble donated the Monastero di San Angel (Monastery of St Angel), one of many Greek monasteries that flourished in this sacred valley. Efforts are being made to turn this fertile valley, famed for its olive oil, into an *agriturismo* destination.

Ionian coastal towns

The further east you travel along the coast from Reggio di Calabria, the poorer and scruffier the towns. While the sea is calm and safe for swimming and the water is crystal clear, the areas around the beaches are unkempt and unappealing and it's often a challenge to access the beach. The main road is on the inland side of the railway line that runs beside the shore, and it's often hard to find a place to cross the line. There are, however, a few towns worth stopping at if cruising the coast.

Bova Marina

Located 13km (8 miles) east of Melito di Porto Salvo, this town boasts several grand pastel-coloured buildings but is mostly blighted by hideous unfinished concrete apartment blocks. From the headland at the eastern end of town there are lovely views of the coast and to Sicily.

ruined houses, along overgrown paths, up and down flights of narrow stairs and through alleys in between empty dilapidated buildings, is indeed a spooky experience. Knowing the story makes it all the more chilling.

Roghudi

Perched precariously on a sliver of hilltop jutting into the dry river bed, Roghudi is quite a sight. While Italian guidebooks maintain that this ramshackle hamlet was abandoned in the 1970s, there were residents living here at the time of writing, and media reports claim it's one of several Aspromonte villages that form the cradle of Calabria's 'Ndrangheta. A visit here is a possible 46km (28-mile) round-trip diversion (via San Lorenzo and Roccaforte del Greco) for those doing the Aspromonte National Park drive (*see pp48–9*). The turn-off is on

Galati

Home to even more shoddily constructed graffiti-covered buildings, this town on Capo Spartivento, 12km (7½ miles) east of Bova Marina, at least enjoys splendid views of the coastline.

Locri

Once one of the most prosperous city-states of Magna Graecia, Locri is now a shabby town of ugly unfinished concrete buildings and terrible traffic-clogged roads. Its saving grace is a pretty lemon-coloured church on the small main square.

Founded in the 7th century BC, Locri was once a great civilisation, admired for its written code of law (the first in the Hellenic world) and its glorious victory in the 6th century BC, with just 10,000 men, over the 130,000-strong Crotonians 25km (15½ miles) north of here. It's now home to the sprawling ancient ruins of **Locri Epizefiri**, which require a great deal of imagination to appreciate. Spread among olive groves and orchards are crumbling temples, the remains of a Graeco-Roman theatre, and a Roman necropolis.

Locri Epizefiri, 3km (1¾ miles) south of Locri town on the E90. Tel: (0964) 390 023. Open: Tue–Sun 9.30am–7pm. Admission charge.

Marina di Gioiosa Jonica and Roccella Jonica

About 4km (2½ miles) north of Siderno and 8km (5 miles) further on respectively, these are two of the more pleasant towns on this stretch of coast. Marina di Gioiosa Jonica has a lively

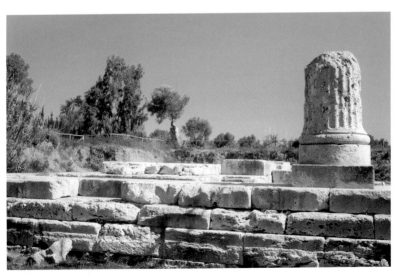

The crumbling ruins of Locri Epizefiri

waterfront with several *gelaterie* and, most surprisingly, a few swish Art Nouveau-style cafés. Roccella Jonica, meanwhile, boasts an attractive seaside promenade lined with palm trees, a captivating castle overlooking the town, and a bustling little piazza where the locals like to linger over drinks at the café tables in the evenings. The beaches here are far more popular with Italian tourists than foreigners, however, who prefer to explore the atmospheric inland villages of Gerace and Stilo.

Siderno

This town, 5km (3 miles) north of Locri, with its drab low-rise apartment blocks would be indistinguishable from its neighbour if it weren't for a smattering

of elegant old buildings, although it suffers from even worse traffic.

Gerace

Gloriously perched atop an impregnable 500m (550yd) long rock formed from sea fossils, and accessed by a steep, tortuous road, Gerace is one of the best-preserved medieval towns in Calabria. Legend has it that, like Stilo, Gerace was established by survivors fleeing 10th-century Saracen raids 10km (6¼ miles) away on the coast at Locri. Archaeologists argue, however, that relics found in Gerace suggest there was a settlement here in the Neolithic Age and later a Roman garrison, but that version isn't nearly as dramatic and Gerace's townsfolk love a

A gate into the old town of Gerace

good story! The town is the location of a number of festivals, held over the spring and summer months.

Locals like to boast that Gerace is the 'Florence of the south' because of its many fine churches, splendid palazzi, cobblestone streets and attractive squares, yet visit Gerace with that comparison in mind and you are likely to be disappointed. The charming town nevertheless warrants a day or two of your time. Once home to 128 churches, Gerace now has just 19, but, of the 72 sights listed in the local tourist brochure, it is the town's gracious churches that are still the most engaging.

Cattedrale dell'Assunta (Cathedral of the Assumption)

On Gerace's main square, Piazza Tribuna, the colossal Norman cathedral is Calabria's largest church. It was established in 1045 by the indomitable Norman conqueror and Duke of Calabria, Robert Guiscard 'the Resourceful', who was instrumental in bringing Roman Christianity to Calabria, and it was later enlarged in 1222 by Frederick II. Inside are 20 columns of granite and marble, each one in a different style, with various decorative capitals. One features *verde antico* marble that is magically able to change colour according to the ambient temperature. Despite the austerity of the well-preserved whitewashed interior, the many arches give the church a distinctly Moorish feel.

The 'Square of the Three Churches'

Open: officially 9am–noon & 3–6pm, but hours are erratic. Free admission.

Piazza delle Tre Chiese (Square of the Three Churches)

A five-minute stroll from the cathedral along Via Caduti sul Lavoro will take you to three impressive churches on this square, which are the **Chiesa del Sacro Cuore** (Church of the Sacred Heart) first on your right, the diminutive 10th-century **San Giovannello** or **San Giovanni Crisostomo** (St John Chrysostom), a Greek Orthodox church on the other side, and the splendid 13th-century **Chiesa di San Francesco d'Assisi** (Church of St Francis of Assisi), which boasts a pretty portal and, inside, an enormous beautiful Baroque marble altar. Concerts are sometimes held here. Unfortunately, the doors aren't always open, but ask around and you'll find someone to let you in.

Drive: Parco Nazionale dell'Aspromonte (Aspromonte National Park)

This rewarding drive passes through breathtakingly beautiful scenery on the way to Calabria's highest mountain. The roads are often overgrown, and you'll see few people other than the occasional shepherd.

Allow one day with stops for lunch and exploration.

From Reggio di Calabria follow the coastal road (SS106/E90) south for 30km (18½ miles). Turn left to visit Pentedattilo, 5km (3 miles) away from Melito di Porto Salvo.

1 Pentedattilo

Take in this atmospheric, semi-abandoned village, dramatically sited beneath the colossal 'five fingers' rock formation (*see pp42–4*).
Return to the coastal road (E90) and continue towards Melito di Porto Salvo, then head inland, following the signs for Chorio, Bagaladi and Gambarie.

2 Chorio

Scenically sited by the River Tuccio, Chorio is the birthplace of St Gaetano Catanoso (*see p42*). From here, the slim road snakes through groves of enormous olive trees and fields of wild flowers.
Follow the signs towards Bagaladi. After about 4km (2½ miles) there is a right turn to Roghudi (see p44), a 46km (28-mile) round-trip detour.

3 Bagaladi

Bagaladi's Monastero di San Angel is one of many Greek monasteries that flourished in this valley. From here the road is tortuous, but worth the views.
Continue along the same road until you reach the turn for Motta San Giovanni.

4 Turn-off to Motta San Giovanni

After this turn-off the landscape changes and plateaus out into lush farmland. Forests of birch, pine and fir form a canopy across the road.
Continue on this road, passing a turn-off to Reggio di Calabria on the left. About 1km (²/₃ mile) later, take the turn-off to Montealto on the right.

5 Montealto

The highlight of Aspromonte, Montealto is the area's highest peak at 1,956m (6,417ft), reached by a sealed road. From here there are spectacular views of Mount Etna to the southeast and dramatic vistas of deep valleys to the north.
Return to the turn-off and continue on.

6 Gambarie

The picnic tables at this charming hamlet make a nice refreshment stop. There's also a trattoria with a terrace.
Take the turn-off on the left to Reggio.

7 Gambarie to San Stefano in Aspromonte

Wooden holiday cottages are nestled among fruit trees, beautiful in spring. After the Mannoli turn-off, Bar Trapani enjoys wonderful mountain vistas, and soon after you'll enjoy splendid views to Sicily.
Continue the descent towards the coast.

8 To San Alessio in Aspromonte and Laganadi

The dilapidated wooden houses in quaint San Alessio have a certain charm. Laganadi's views to the village across the valley are magnificent.
Continue the descent. At Gallico, take the signposted turn for Reggio.

Drive: Parco Nazionale dell'Aspromonte (Aspromonte National Park)

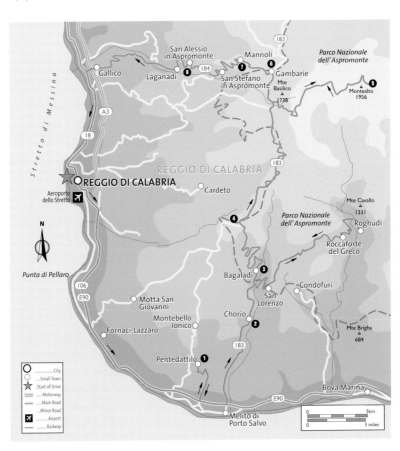

O	City
o	Small Town
☆	Start of Drive
	Motorway
	Main Road
	Minor Road
✈	Airport
	Railway

Stilo

Sprawled across the lower slopes of a squat rock called Monte Consolino 15km (9¼ miles) inland from the coastal 106/E90 road, the small village of Stilo is famous for two things: **La Cattolica**, an exquisite 10th-century Byzantine church, and the **Ribusa Palio**, a medieval fair on the first Sunday in August, featuring banner-waving 'knights' on horseback competing in equestrian tournaments, jesters, fortune-tellers, processions and banquets with court music.

Founded in the 7th century by coastal inhabitants looking for a safe haven from the pillaging Saracens, Stilo would become a key city in Calabria's history, securing autonomy under the Normans and maintaining some power and influence throughout the periods of Swabian, Angevin and Aragonese rule. It was the birthplace of a number of revered Calabrians, including artist Francesco Cozza and cartographer Domenico Vigliarolo, inventor of a sundial with a compass.

Handily placed for a visit on the way to Serra San Bruno, and accessed via a meandering mountain road, Stilo has several sights worth seeing including the eerie ruins of a Norman castle, a number of splendid churches, a pretty Arabic-influenced fountain (Fontana Gebbia) and the remains of majestic medieval walls and town gates.

The first church you'll see on the left as you enter town is the Renaissance-era **Chiesa San Francesco** (Church of St Francis), dating from 1450 and part of a complex of Renaissance-style buildings from the period. Further along, on Piazza San Giovanni, the late Renaissance **Chiesa San Giovanni** (Church of St John), built in 1625, is in a Baroque style typical of Calabrian churches.

If you backtrack a little and stroll up Via Tommaso Campanella and then along Via Luigi Cunsolo, you'll arrive at the imposing **Duomo**, constructed in 1300 and featuring a Roman-Gothic portal and a precious altar inside. In the labyrinthine streets behind the cathedral is the 17th-century **Chiesa San Domenico** (Church of St Dominic). Most people, however, make a beeline for the iconic La Cattolica. And on the other side of Monte Consolino, **Bivongi**, famous for its sweet wine, is home to another charming Byzantine church.

La Cattolica

The exquisite 10th-century Byzantine church that clings to the slopes of Monte Consolino is without doubt the main reason most people visit Stilo. In an architectural style more typically found in Greece, it's the only church of its kind in Calabria and it's the incongruity of La Cattolica's location in this mountainous part of southern Italy that is so alluring.

Scramble up to the rise above the cobblestone path and you can capture a picture-postcard image of the captivating church framed by

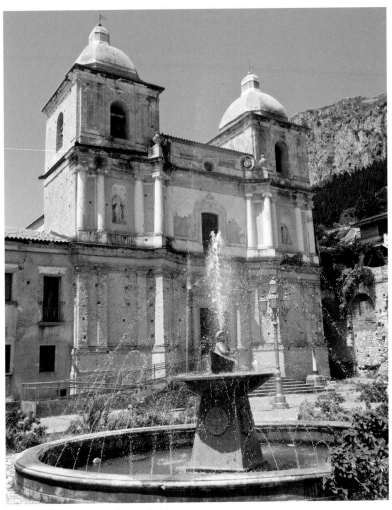

Stilo's grand Duomo with its Roman-Gothic entrance

enormous agave cacti with the pretty town and its sand-coloured roof tiles in the background. Inside you can also appreciate vivid Byzantine frescoes and a charming interior, illuminated by windows in the domes.

There is a kiosk and café tables off the car park before the church, from where you can enjoy stupendous views over the village and valley.

Via Cattolica, near Piazza San Giovanni. Tel: (0964) 776 006 (office at castle). Open: daily 8am–8pm. Free admission.

Vibo Valentia province

Vibo Valentia is Calabria's smallest province but it's also its luckiest, blessed with the region's liveliest provincial capital, its most beautiful towns in Tropea and Pizzo, enchanting forests and churches at Serra San Bruno, spectacular coastline and beaches, and a gastronomic scene that's the envy of the region. Bordering Catanzaro to the north and east, Reggio di Calabria to the south, and the turquoise Tyrrenhian Sea to the west, compact Vibo Valentia offers a fine taste of the best Calabria has to offer.

The coastline is skirted by long stretches of sand, crescent beaches hugged by craggy rocks, and sheltered fishing coves carved from sheer cliffs.

The alluring hilltop towns of Tropea and Pizzo have an abundance of charm, boasting warrens of atmospheric lanes, pretty palazzi perched on a cliff's edge,

Tropea's beaches are some of the best in the region

gorgeous sea vistas from belvederes, and delicious gelato and tartufo celebrated all over Italy.

Capo Vaticano serves up more splendid beaches backed by family-focused resorts and campsites. Inland, undulating slopes are concealed by olive groves and grapevines, and lush mountains are ideal for hiking and mountain biking.

HISTORY

Vibo Valentia city was once the Greek colony Hipponion, founded in the 7th century BC by inhabitants of Locri, the great Magna Graecia city on Calabria's east coast. Hipponion thrived for several hundred years until its cocky residents declared war on their former homeland. As a result, in 388 BC Hipponion was invaded by Dionysius the Elder, Tyrant of Syracuse, its citizens were deported to Sicily, and a destroyed city was handed to Locri. The Carthaginians helped the exiles return and rebuild in 378 BC, but the following

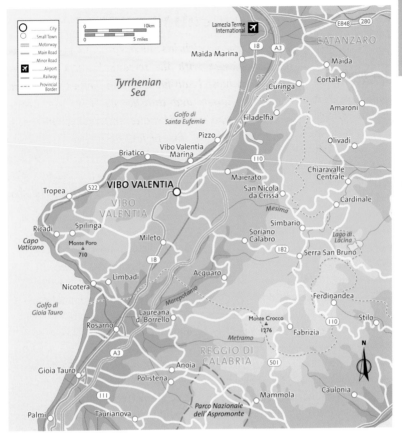

year Hipponion would be occupied again, this time by the Bruttii, the native people of the land, now former slaves, rebels and refugees who'd been hiding in the wilderness until they rose to take control of most of Calabria.

The Romans arrived and Hipponion became Hipponium, and then Valentia when designated a Latin colony in 194 BC, flourishing after the Popilian Way was constructed, connecting it to Rome and Sicily. A glorious theatre and villas with mosaic floors were built, grapevines and olives were cultivated, and fishing developed. Vibo declined with the Roman Empire's fall. Revitalised after the Normans arrived in 1070 and built the castle on the old Acropolis ruins, it was renamed Monteleone in 1235, and developed on the orders of Frederick II, Holy Roman Emperor and King of Sicily. The name Vibo Valentia was restored by the Fascists in 1928.

VIBO VALENTIA CITY

Elegantly sprawled across the mountain slopes with vistas downhill through the streets to the sea, Vibo Valentia is one of Calabria's most vibrant cities. An important commercial, agricultural and manufacturing hub, the city's affluence is evident in Corso Vittorio Emanuele III's chic boutiques, the restoration of grand edifices, real estate developments, and the demeanour and dress of Vibo's well-heeled citizens who congregate at the imposing cathedral for Sunday Mass, and gather for the city's evening *passeggiata*, one of the liveliest in Calabria, starting around 5pm on Corso Vittorio Emanuele III.

Begin exploring Vibo at the impressively opulent **Duomo** (*Piazza San Leoluca*), then follow Via San Leoluca to the stairs near Palazzo Daffina and continue along the renovated promenade that's home to beautifully restored palazzi before stopping for coffee at atmospheric **Bar del Corso**. Hike up the hill to visit the **Chiesa dello Spirito Santo** (Church of the Holy Spirit, *Via Gagliardi Caterina*) and the picturesque streets of Via Pasquale Galluppi, Via Roma, Via Vito Capialbi and Via Michele Morelli.

Around Via Gesù and Via Jazzolino there are several interesting churches; look out for carvings around the church portals. The renovated lemon-painted **Conservatorio Musicali di Stato** (State Musical Conservatory) is on Largo Bisogni. Take in the picturesque scene of pastel-coloured buildings, ornate balconies and old-fashioned lampposts towards Via Ettore Capialbi and Corso Umberto I, which lead to Via Roma and Corso Vittorio Emanuele III.

Vibo Valentia Marina, a ten-minute drive away, was established as a harbour in the 3rd century BC. Vital for the region's thriving tuna-fishing industry, it's a key transit point for the Aeolian Islands and a busy yachting hub. At weekends and during summer the seafood restaurants and *gelaterie* here are crammed with tourists and locals.

Il Castello Normanno-Svevo (Norman-Swabian Castle)

Established by Roger the Norman in 1070 in a strategic position looking over the valley and coast below, this imposing castle began life as a watchtower. A town soon developed at the foot of the hill, so the Swabians, who took over from the Normans, strengthened the castle, adding structures that gave it its current form.

The Angevins at the end of the 13th century fortified the building further with a buttress and immense doorway, added a chapel and installed a cistern. Close to devastation following the 1783 earthquake, the fortress was abandoned until the Bourbons rebuilt it in 1858 as a prison. Two years later, following an uprising, it was extensively damaged and once more abandoned.

In recent years the castle has been renovated and rooms have been opened up to create space and light for the Museo Archeologico Nazionale Vito

Capialbi (*see below*). The castle is connected to the *centro storico* by a series of 18th-century stairways and is well signposted.
Via Castello 1. Tel: (0963) 433 50.
Open: Tue–Sun 9am–7pm.
Free admission.

Museo Archeologico Nazionale Vito Capialbi (Vito Capialbi National Archaeology Museum)

This excellent museum was named after celebrated archaeologist and scholar Vito Capialbi, who gathered most of the collection on display and then donated it. It includes treasures from ancient Hipponion up to the time of the Bruttian conquest.

Most relics were found at sacred sites, such as Scimbia and Cofino, and include votive offerings along with splendid ceramics, perfume bottles, earrings, hair slides, mirrors and decorated vases. Some brilliantly preserved warriors' bronze helmets demonstrate the technical skill of Hipponion's 6th-century BC artisans. Also impressive are marble statues, models of Greek temples, and temple panels depicting mythical scenes. The most precious object is a wafer-thin gold sheet inscribed with Greek text dating from the 5th century BC. There have been only six others found in the Greek world.
Contact details as castle above.
Admission charge.

The Museo Archeologico Nazionale Vito Capialbi is located in a Norman castle

Cathedrals and churches

One of the constants of exploring Calabria is the proliferation of churches and how these churches are central – literally and figuratively – to the lives of the inhabitants of the villages and towns. Many are surprising: a modest exterior can belie the beautiful mosaics and paintings within. Others, in tiny hilltop villages, have spires that can be seen several kilometres away.

The austere Byzantine-era churches dotting Calabria are the most unusual. The greatest of these

Interior detail of the Church of San Marco in Rossano

churches is the modest La Cattolica di Stilo (*see pp50–51*). At the time of its founding, between the 10th and 11th centuries, Stilo was a centre for religion. The fine red-brick construction follows a Greek cross plan with three apses arranged around a central dome, and the church's hillside location gives visitors a lovely view down to Stilo. The interior was once completely covered in frescoes, but the remaining faded paintings that still adorn the walls are well worth inspecting.

The cathedral in the city of Reggio di Calabria is the largest religious building in the region, with a neo-Romanesque façade and Gothic influences inside. It measures 93m (305ft) in length and more than 26m (85ft) in width, and it is 21m (69ft) high. The structure is impressive, made even more so by the fact that it was completely rebuilt after the 1908 earthquake rendered the old church unsalvageable. While churches had existed on this spot since 1453, they had seen various repairs and restorations over the years, including in the aftermath of the 1783 earthquake. The façade's four towers with little cupolas are a striking

La Cattolica at Stilo is the most famous church in Calabria

feature, as are the intricate bronze entrance doors, which were commissioned in 1988. The three-aisled interior is home to some great works, notably the marble pulpit by Francesco Jerace and, at the end of the right aisle, a 19th-century canvas by Carlo Maria Minaldi depicting the consecration of St Stephen, Bishop of Reggio, by St Paul.

Gerace was once famous for having well over 100 churches, and today this town, set dramatically on a steep mound, still has the largest Norman cathedral in Calabria, as well as the notably exquisite Baroque altar in the Chiesa di San Francesco d'Assisi, dating from the 13th century. Also in the town are the small San Giovannello church dating from the 10th century and the Greek Santa Maria del Mastro (1083).

In Rossano, the cathedral, rebuilt after the 1836 earthquake, houses a notable 9th-century Byzantine fresco, *Madonna Achiropita*. Next door, the Museo Diocesano (Diocese Museum) is home to the *Purple Codex* (*Codex Purpureus Rossanensis*), a unique 6th-century illustrated book on the life of Christ. Somewhat less elaborate is the Chiesa di San Marco, a modest and compact Byzantine church dating from around the 10th century.

While there are several churches in Paola, the nearby Santuario di San Francesco di Paola, located in a ravine above the town, is an important venue for pilgrims as it's the spiritual home of Calabria's patron saint. The façade dates from the 16th century and the saint's relics are located in the Chiesa di Santa Maria degli Angeli, next door.

TROPEA

Dubbed 'the Positano of the South' because of its elegant palazzi with balconies dripping with bougainvillea, steep narrow streets, spectacular sea vistas and superb sandy beaches, Tropea is Calabria's most beautiful city and its most popular tourist destination – and deservedly so.

Stunningly situated on the Tyrrenhian Sea, at the foot of Monte Poro, which separates the Gulf of Gioia Tauro from the Gulf of Santa Eufemia, Tropea sits atop an enormous Miocenic sandstone rock, known locally as La Rupe ('the cliff') or Il Scoglio ('the rock'). The city's elegant old sandstone palazzi and somewhat crumbling apartments seamlessly blend with the sheer cliffs, which dramatically drop down to the coastal road and sea below. From the sandy beach it appears as if Tropea has been carved out of the very rock it's perched upon.

To add to the drama of the setting, another smaller rock, L'Isola Bella ('the beautiful island'), strikingly juts into the sea, with the splendid convent **Santa Maria dell'Isola** standing on top. Located in a luxuriant garden that sprawls across the top of the outcrop, the convent was established under the auspices of the Benedictine Abbey of Montecassino, near Naples, in 1077, to which it had been assigned by Pope Urban II. It was consecrated in 1397.

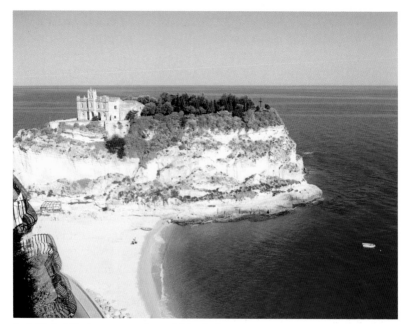

Santa Maria dell'Isola punctuates the small 'island' off Tropea

A house of religious worship had stood on this spot since the 4th century, when a Byzantine monastery was founded by St Basil the Great, who was responsible for hundreds of monastic communities in Calabria. Like so many of the region's great buildings, the old convent was devastated during the 1908 earthquake and rebuilt in a Gothic style. It was closed for restoration at the time of writing.

Legend has it that Hercules founded Tropea when he stopped to delight in a garden here, and so taken was he with the area that he built a port and named the place after himself: Porto Ercole. Indeed, this story is supported by the ancient Roman author Pliny the Elder. Another tale, meanwhile, has a victorious Sextus Pompeius, having won a battle against Octavius Augustus, celebrate his triumph (*trofaea*) by founding a town: Trofaea.

The Greeks, Romans, Byzantines, Saracens, Normans, Swabians, Angevins, Aragonese and Bourbons all settled in Tropea at some point, but it was during the Norman occupation that the city assumed a strategic maritime role under Ruggero II Guiscardo, Duke of Calabria and Puglia. Indeed, another story attributes Tropea's name to the words *tropee* and *trupia*, still used by local mariners to refer to the strong, dangerous currents that characterise the sea around Tropea.

Traces of many different historical periods are much more apparent in

Tropea's harbour

Tropea's well-preserved centre than in other towns in Calabria because Tropea managed to escape the degree of earthquake damage that they experienced. During the Renaissance, Tropea was a literary centre and enjoyed a period of splendour that is still evident in the elegant palazzi that belonged to aristocrats, the coats of arms that still grace some buildings, the attractive cobblestone courtyards with pretty fountains, the grand 11th-century Norman cathedral, the city's myriad churches, and the massive Baroque, Arab and Gothic granite and sandstone portals around the old town.

Exploring the enchanting warren of alleyways that is Tropea's old town is one of the reasons to stay in the city, rather than by the beach. One of the great pleasures is waking early in the morning for a saunter through the tranquil pedestrian-only streets to one of the belvederes to take in the view of sparkling sea, visible from a number of vantage points. A stroll through the breezy lanes in the late afternoon when the buildings take on a golden-orange hue is something of a ritual with the locals, always including a gelato or beer stop. And, once more, a wander after dinner is a must, when the moodily lit

The cobbled streets of Tropea in the late afternoon

CIPOLLA DI TROPEA

Italy's most prized onion comes from the coast between Capo Vaticano and Vibo Valentia and is commonly known as the Tropea onion (*cipolla di Tropea*). One of the sweetest varieties of onion in the world, it's found all over Calabria, its distinctive deep-red colour (and pink centre) and slightly oval shape a fixture of every fruit and vegetable stand and souvenir shop. While others have tried to replicate the flavour of the onion, locals say that it's the soil, climate and generations of experience that make it unique. A simple pasta of spaghetti and Tropea onions is a local favourite dish and the *marmalade* or *confetture* made with it is great on toast or with cheese and is a scrumptious culinary souvenir.

lanes and gleaming cobblestones will remind you of Rome.

The unique local cuisine and lively dining scene is another reason to linger and consider making Tropea your base for exploring Calabria. No other town has so many superb restaurants, from cheap family pizzerie with rickety wooden tables set up in an alleyway, to more elegant trattorie serving freshly caught swordfish and other exquisitely prepared regional specialities.

Tropea boasts two beautiful beaches: Mar Piccolo ('Little Sea') and Spiaggia della Rotonda beneath the convent immediately below town, and Mare Grande ('Big Sea') and Spiaggia del Convento on the other side of the convent. Both are within walking distance, accessible by stairs from Largo Duomo. Mar Piccolo is a ten-minute walk and Mare Grande a further five minutes away. There is another set of stairs that would take you straight to Mare Grande beneath Largo Porta Vaticana, but these were closed for restoration at the time of writing. The beach at Parghelia, on the other side of the port, is best reached by car. There are lidos on all the beaches where you can hire sunbeds and umbrellas, but there is also free beach space to spread out your towel.

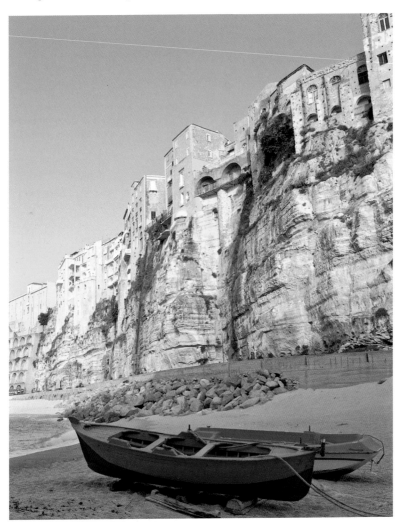

Tropea's cliff-top buildings are a dramatic backdrop to the main beach

Walk: Tropea

This easy saunter around Tropea's enchanting centro storico takes in the main attractions of the old town, atmospheric alleyways, marvellous palazzi, magnificent churches and the alluring sea vistas from its popular belvederes.

The walk takes about an hour, longer with stops for gelato and beers. It's best to begin it in the late afternoon.

Start and finish on the main square, Piazza Ercole.

1 Piazza Ercole

This lovely square is lined with *gelaterie* and cafés with terraces, where you can try Tropea's famed gelato.
From Piazza Ercole follow Corso Vittorio Emanuele to Piazza Mercato to visit Chiesa di Santa Caterina.

2 Chiesa di Santa Caterina (Church of St Catherine)

Following the destruction of the Dominican church in the 1783 earthquake, restoration work incorporated the old church ruins within the new structure. Inside are splendid paintings.
Return along Corso Vittorio Emanuele to Piazza Ercole. Turn right on Via Roma to get to Largo Duomo.

3 Il Duomo (Cathedral)

This imposing Norman cathedral is one of Calabria's finest, bearing the marks of several historical periods. Two unexploded American bombs from World War II are displayed by the main door – with a grateful prayer to the Madonna attached!
Cross Largo Duomo to admire the views of the port and sea. Return to the corner of Largo Duomo and Via Boiano, and follow this alley to Largo Galluppi.

4 Largo Galluppi and Largo Municipio

Largo Galluppi was named after philosopher Pasquale Galluppi (1770–1846), born nearby on Largo di Francia. Note the impressive portals, one Baroque and one Gothic. Largo Municipio is surrounded by splendid buildings, including Congrega dei Nobili, Ex Convento dei Francescani Conventuali, and Ex Collegio dei PP Gesuiti.
Cross Largo Padre V M Netta to Chiesa del Gesù, on your right.

5 Chiesa del Gesù (Church of Jesus)

This imposing 18th-century Jesuit church was built upon the ruins of a cathedral dating from early Christian and Byzantine times. Inside are precious relics, an ornate Baroque altar and valuable paintings.

Follow narrow Via d'Aquino across Piazza Toraldo Grimaldi and along Via Aragona. Turn right on Dardano, cross Vico delle Pentite, turn left on Largo Sannio and right on Via Pelliccia.

6 Largo Migliarese

This belvedere boasts the most spectacular views in Tropea, looking directly on to Mar Piccolo ('Little Sea') and the stunning Santa Maria dell'Isola convent on the headland.

Follow Corso Vittorio Emanuele towards Piazza Ercole, then turn right on Via Pietro Vianeo to Via Indipendenza.

7 Largo Villetta

This small square off Largo Porta Vaticana is *the* spot to watch the sunset. Buy a beer from the café-bar and join the locals on a bench for this daily ritual. On a clear day you can see the volcanic island of Stromboli, but, if you can't see that, just take in the splendid views of Santa Maria dell'Isola on the craggy outcrop above the aquamarine sea.

Cross the square to Via Indipendenza.

8 Via Indipendenza

This atmospheric lane is lined with delightful shops crammed with delicious local specialities such as Tropea onions and liquorice liqueurs.

Take time to browse on the way back to Piazza Ercole.

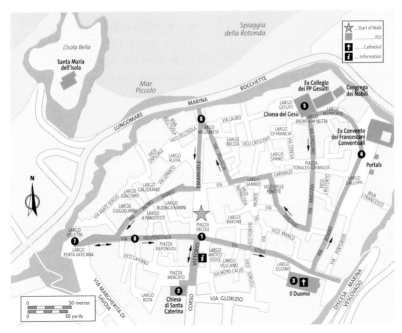

CAPO VATICANO

The coast south between Tropea and Capo Vaticano boasts some of Calabria's best beaches, and on the other side of the cape, on the Golfo di Gioia Tauro, is one of the region's most dramatic stretches of coastline, best appreciated on a drive from Nicotera in the direction of Tropea.

There are dozens of pristine beaches with crystal-clear water, from long, wide stretches of sand to tiny crescent beaches within pretty coves protected by craggy rocks and sheer cliffs. There are lidos all along here where umbrellas and sunbeds can be rented for the day, and it's also possible to find the occasional stretch of free sand. The problem? Unless you're staying at one of the beach resorts or caravan- and campsites dotted along the coast, you'll have a difficult time accessing the beach. There are few parking spaces and in summer you'll have a very long walk. Whatever you do, avoid the area in August, when the whole of Italy is on holiday.

The good news is that Capo Vaticano's proximity to the mountains means that when you tire of the beach (or can't get access to it) you can head into the hills for walking, hiking, horse riding and mountain biking.

PIZZO

Pizzo is one of Calabria's prettiest towns, with its pastel-painted palazzi and charming red-roofed residences sprawled across a headland that's nearly as dramatic as its rival Tropea's. Known locally as 'La Pizzu', this alluring coastal town on the Tyrrhenian Sea north of Vibo Valentia is a delight to explore.

But while many of its backstreets, such as Via Savoia, Via Musolino and Via Roma, are atmospheric and authentic –

A statue in Pizzo's main square

you'll see washing strung from lines, smell mouthwatering aromas that waft from kitchens and hear families sitting down for a meal together – sadly, the main shopping street of Corso Garibaldi has been given over to a few too many tacky souvenir shops.

The attractive main square, Piazza della Repubblica, is lined with *gelaterie* specialising in Pizzo's beloved chocolate tartufo dessert in addition to delicious gelato, but during the summer you'll see more tourists than locals partaking. Wander just one street back from the piazza and you'll discover down-to-earth trattorie and *enoteche* more deserving of your attention.

The sea vistas from the belvedere off Piazza della Repubblica and from Piazza Musolino are spectacular. From Musolino a path and some steps take you down to the palm-lined Lungomare Cristoforo Colombo and a small beach on the southern side of the headland, and on the northern side a tiny sheltered fishing cove.

Pizzo may not boast the dozen or so churches that Tropea does, but there are a few worthwhile attractions. The white-and-lemon 17th-century **Chiesa dell'Immacolata** (Church of the Immaculate Conception) on the main piazza boasts an ornate interior and beautiful paintings and is home to an illuminated statue of the Madonna. The diminutive cliff-top 15th-century Aragonese **Murat Castle** (*Tel: (0963) 532 523. Open: daily 9am–1pm & 3–7pm. Admission charge*), accessed

The road winding down to Pizzo's waterfront

from nearby Piazza Musolino, is where French General Joachim Murat was shot after an attempt to provoke a revolt against the Bourbon rulers in 1815.

Pizzo's most unusual sight is the 15th-century (or 17th – the date is disputed) **Chiesetta di Piedigrotta** (literally, 'Little Church of the Foot of the Grotto', *www.chiesadipiedigrotta.it. Open: daily 9am–1pm & 3–7.30pm. Admission charge*), where a church was dug out of a recess in the rock by sailors who had miraculously survived a shipwreck and been washed ashore on this spot. In the 19th century two local artists, Angelo Barone and his son Alfonso, sculpted statues from the volcanic rock to create scenes from the Gospels and lives of the saints.

Statue of San Bruno at the monastery

SERRA SAN BRUNO

The wonderful drive to Serra San Bruno – along narrow, winding roads skirted with wild flowers, shaded by dense canopies of fir and pine, through picturesque emerald pastures – is easily as pleasurable as an actual visit to this somnolent mountain town, famous for its fairy-tale Carthusian monastery, beautiful churches and leafy forest walking trails.

While Serra San Bruno, or 'St Bruno's Greenhouse', is accessible from Vibo Valentia city in the northwest (about 25km/15½ miles: from the A3 take the Pizzo Calabro exit and SS110, or the Serra San Bruno exit and SS182), the easterly route from Stilo in Reggio di Calabria province, also using the SS110, must be one of Calabria's most spectacular drives. It is also one of the

most fragrant – this is a drive you'll want to do with the windows down because the area is so aromatic, heady with the scents of wild flowers and pine.

It's used less often than the westerly roads, so you'll see few other travellers, but do take care. The road up to the plateau is narrow and tortuous in parts, and it's not unusual to turn a corner and suddenly come across a parked car taking up one lane of the road. Look closely and you'll see the car's occupants, arms laden with empty plastic water bottles, filling them with fresh, mountain spring water from the roadside fountains. Make sure you stop and try some of the water yourself. It's icy!

Once at Serra San Bruno, park the car and take a stroll. The *centro storico*, known as the Terravecchia (literally 'old land'), developed in the 11th century after the monastery of Serra San Bruno was established here, while the 'new' area, built after the 1783 earthquake, is called Spinetto. There is an attractive main street of delightful, historical, two-storey houses in Spinetto, and half a dozen splendid old Baroque churches, mostly 18th century, scattered between Spinetto and the Terravecchia. These include Chiesa San Rocco, Chiesa Matrice, Chiesa Maria SS dei Sette Dolori, Chiesa SS Assunta di Terravecchia, Chiesa SS Assunta di Spinetto, and the two main attractions that most people make the pilgrimage to Serra San Bruno to see: **La Certosa di Serra San Bruno** and the **Santuario di Santa Maria nel Bosco**, prettily set within the forest (*see pp68–9*). Most of the churches are made of granite and many feature beautiful wooden crosses made by the wood and granite (and also wrought-iron) artisans for which Serra San Bruno was famous.

If you arrive in the late afternoon on a weekend during the warmer months, you can join the Italians in their *passeggiata* from the town centre along a path running beside the road to La Certosa di Serra San Bruno, and then along a leafy path that runs through the forest to the Santuario di Santa Maria nel Bosco. The *passeggiata* is a fun ritual anywhere, but it's especially enjoyable here because of the tranquil natural setting.

Families ride bicycles, and flirty young couples saunter hand in hand along the forest trail, visitors ride a small tourist train or rent a horse and buggy that takes them on the shaded road beside the trails, while elderly locals lean their bicycles against the tall trees in front of La Certosa di Serra San Bruno and take it all in from wooden park benches.

Vibo Valentia province

A walk in the park at Serra San Bruno

La Certosa di Serra San Bruno (Carthusian Monastery of Serra San Bruno)

The Carthusian monks are hermits who live a contemplative life in solitude and silence dedicated to God. This splendid monastery was established in 1091 by the monk St Bruno of Cologne, founder of the Carthusian Order. Built on land given to him by the Norman Count Ruggiero for the purpose of building Italy's first hermitage or charterhouse, it was Europe's second such institution. The first was built when the saint founded the Carthusian Order in 1084 in Chartreuse, near Grenoble, France. The original Italian building was destroyed by earthquakes, and the current building was constructed in 1900 in a Gothic style.

A museum was established to raise the funds necessary to maintain the monastery, and it provides an insight

ONE PIG, 12 MONTHS OF HAPPINESS

'He who kills a pig is happy for a year; he who marries is happy for a day.' Variations of this saying are heard everywhere around Calabria and other areas of the south. While the marriage jibe is either amusing or offensive depending on your point of view, the message about the pig is instructive. In Calabria, where famine was commonplace until recently, the killing of a pig was – and still is – a major event. *Every* part of the pig is used, from snout to tail, and the prosciutto, *salumi* and other products made from the pig can last until the next pig meets its maker 12 months down the road.

into the history of the Carthusian Order, the monastery and the life of the monks. This is the only part of the monastery that can be accessed. Visitors can view a cell similar to that of a Carthusian monk, while another room has been set up to resemble the church where the monks celebrate the liturgy. Within the grounds of the monastery is the beautiful granite 16th-century façade of the old church.

Museo della Certosa, Corso da Certosa 1. Tel: (0963) 706 08. Open: daily 10am–1pm & 3–6pm. Groups by appointment only; it's advisable for all visitors to call ahead as opening hours are erratic. Admission charge.

Santuario di Santa Maria nel Bosco (Sanctuary of St Mary in the Woods)

A short stroll from the monastery along a lovely trail through a forest of ancient fir trees and beeches is the sanctuary

Santuario di Santa Maria nel Bosco

where St Bruno spent the last decade of his life. You can't miss it. There are a couple of cafés at the entrance, horses for rent, and in summer a funfair set up for the thousands of tourists and pilgrims who visit throughout the season.

On the first square is St Bruno's Pond, also known as the 'Lake of Miracles', a spring featuring a statue of the saint, where it's said he used to immerse himself in water as a form of repentance. From here, a granite stairway, charmingly overgrown with grass and moss, leads to the sanctuary, which after the 1783 earthquake was rebuilt upon the ruins of a church where St Bruno and his monks used to pray. Inside the church (under restoration at the time of writing) are some works of art and a 19th-century wooden statue of St Mary. Opposite the sanctuary is St Bruno's 'dormitory', where the monk sought refuge and where he is now buried.

Vibo Valentia province

The Museo della Certosa is the only part of the Carthusian Monastery open to the public

Catanzaro province

Catanzaro province covers part of the sole of Italy's boot, stretching from the provinces of Crotone and Cosenza in the north, along the Gulf of Squillace, to the province of Reggio di Calabria in the south and Vibo Valentia to the west. It may be Calabria's least engaging province for travellers, with a coastline of sprawling cookie-cutter holiday developments and scruffy campsites, but it boasts the gorgeous green fields and thick forests of the Sila Piccola, and a small mountainous area of enchanting hilltop villages.

Thought to have been named Kata'Antheros by the ancient Greeks ('Hill Hanging with Flowers'), Catanzaro's mountains were once thick with mulberry trees and blanketed with the flowering broom shrub. Catanzaro's citizens still proudly boast that in the 15th century their city was the silk capital of the world, due to the thriving mulberry forests and the area's success at breeding silkworms. Celebrated for its fine linens and laces worn by nobles and used by the Vatican, Catanzaro saw merchants arriving from all over Europe to buy its beautiful textiles and exquisite handwoven brocades.

Catanzaro city

Catanzaro was ruled by the Aragonese in the 15th century and by the Spanish in the 16th. In 1528, the city's nobles courageously rebelled against the occupiers. The Spanish viceroy Pedro Alarcón de Mendoza fought back with 11,000 troops, leading to a long, spirited siege. Emperor Charles V called the city *Magnifica et Fidelissima* (magnificent and faithful) and bestowed upon Catanzaro the rare distinction of a specially minted coin.

Sprawled across three rocky hills – the Hill of St Rocco, the Hill of St John and the Episcopate's Hill – the city would be attractive if it weren't for the widespread graffiti, the unsightly ring road and the colossal concrete and steel bridges over the deep Fiumarella Valley. One of the bridges, Fiumarella Viaduct, was designed in 1960 by the great Italian engineer Riccardo Morandi (1902–89).

Once a grand city of churches, palaces and ancient buildings, Catanzaro lost much of its elegant architecture – and population – in the earthquakes of 1783 and 1832. As a result, apart from the charming, compact old centre, the city is an architectural mishmash, although a short stroll through the *centro storico* pays off with a labyrinthine heart that's a delight to explore – provided you ignore the graffiti everywhere.

Catanzaro's main attractions include the elegant 15th-century **Palazzo de' Nobili**, now the Town Hall, and several splendid surviving churches including the recently restored **Chiesa di San Giovanni Battista** (1502) at the main entrance to the *centro storico* off Piazza Matteotti. A five-minute walk up the hill is the diminutive 11th-century Byzantine church of **Sant'Omobono** and, off the square opposite, the **Basilica dell'Immacolata**. In a further ten minutes, on a street off Corso Mazzini, just before Piazza Cavour, you will reach the 15th-century **Chiesa del Santissimo Rosario**, which boasts a beautiful Renaissance façade and nave inside.

Opposite, on Piazza Duomo, the modern neoclassical **cathedral** was reconstructed after the original Norman cathedral (1121) was damaged by earthquakes, and then destroyed by bombing in 1943. Also worth a look are

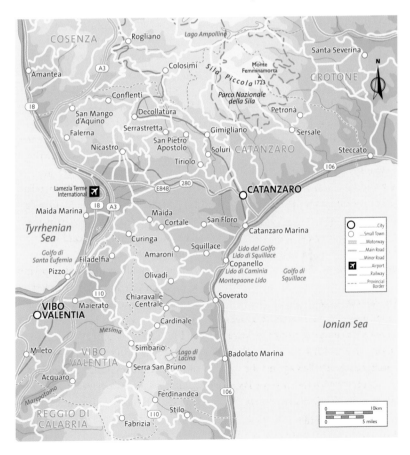

the remains of the **Norman castle** and the two city gates, Porta di San Agostino and Porta di Stratò, all that is left of the medieval walls.

Gimigliano, Tiriolo and surrounds

Precariously perched on a hilltop and spectacularly situated in a valley of deep ravines and thick woods, the gorgeous village of Gimigliano is worth the harrowing drive along a winding road through the mountains northwest of Catanzaro. Take care, especially at weekends, when the roads are popular with kamikaze motorbike riders and locals who stop to fill water bottles at the natural springs.

With pretty pastel-coloured houses in pink, yellow, orange and terracotta, and a charming church in the centre, the village is divided into an upper and lower town, the upper older and more fascinating, the lower dramatically situated on a high rock. It's well worth visiting, if you can find a parking spot outside Gimigliano (impossible on a Sunday afternoon, when the whole valley turns up for the evening *passeggiata*). Alternatively, try to stop on the Gimigliano–Tiriolo road a couple of kilometres away between the village and Soluri to enjoy magnificent views of it through the canopy of trees. The equally enchanting village of Tiriolo, with a pretty little piazza and small church, is 9km (5½ miles) south of Gimigliano.

A further 13km (8 miles) north of Tiriolo along a particularly picturesque road are the villages of **San Pietro Apostolo** and **Serrastretta**. Here, local women have set up looms in an attempt to revive the tradition of weaving cotton, linen and yarn from the local broom flower. The textured cloths are stunning.

From Serrastretta, you can continue northwest for about 35km (22 miles) via Decollatura and Conflenti along a meandering road to **San Mango d'Aquino**, another charming village that spills down a hillside. Alternatively, from Tiriolo head southwest for 7km (4¼ miles) to the E848. As you drive down the mountain, you'll enjoy magnificent views of both of Calabria's coasts, with the Ionian Sea to the east and the Tyrrhenian Sea to the west.

Squillace

Blink and you'll miss the turn-off to Squillace, 6km (3¾ miles) southwest of Catanzaro Marina. A twisting road, skirted by enormous cacti bursting with yellow flowers, takes you up to the village, dramatically sprawled across the hill. Only a few of its 28 beautiful churches survived the 1783 earthquake. Off the main square, the cathedral and the Norman *castello* are worth a look. If they're not open, ask the locals sitting on the church steps if you can take a peek inside. Equally compelling are the views of the sea and coast from a lookout on the road into town.

Local guardians will let you have a look inside Squillace's Duomo

San Floro and Cortale

Once celebrated for their handmade silk brocades, the villages of San Floro, 12km (7½ miles) north of Squillace, and Cortale, 18km (11 miles) northwest, are working to revive their weaving traditions. Sitting prettily on hilltops overlooking a lovely valley, both villages have municipalities that encourage enterprising locals to cultivate mulberry trees and experiment with silk-making techniques. In San Floro a small silk museum and factory are being developed, and, at Cortale, Dal Baco alla Seta ('From Worm to Silk') sells splendid hand-woven silk bedspreads, curtains and cushion covers.

Soverato

Back on the coast, between Copanello and Soverato, the squeaky cream-sand beaches are superb. Soverato is one of the most affluent and attractive towns on this stretch, with a splendid 16th-century watchtower, a wide seaside promenade shaded by palm trees and oleander bushes, and busy garden pizzerie. The main street of Corso Umberto I is lined with grand buildings and the elegant **Chiesa del Rosario**. On the last Sunday of the month, it's closed for the lively Fiera Espositiva dell'Antiquariato (antique fair), which is worth visiting.

Calabrian arts and crafts

Calabria boasts rich traditions of arts and crafts, influenced over the centuries by the ancient Greeks, Romans, Arabs and Normans. Handed down from generation to generation, many traditions started to die out following Calabrians' mass emigration. In recent years, however, there has been some reappraisal and rejuvenation of traditional arts and crafts production. Originally created for everyday use in and around the house, Calabria's splendid arts and crafts are now highly coveted by locals and visitors alike.

A hand-painted preserve jar

History

Calabrians have produced arts and crafts since prehistory, creating fine textiles, woodwork, wickerwork, ceramics and pottery. Archaeologists uncovered clay pottery shards at sites around Bova Marina, dating back not only to the classical Greek period but as far as early Neolithic times, which were the subject of study due to their technological advancement.

A wealth of exquisite bronzework, pottery, ceramics, glass and jewellery from Greek and Roman times was found in Sybaris and is still being unearthed. Ironwork was practised at Trebisacce, where an ancient forge, dating from the Bronze Age, was found in the acropolis of Broglio, along with cup fragments. It's thought that this was where the lathe was used for the first time in Italy.

Pottery and ceramics

Most of the traditional pottery-making techniques still used date from the ancient Magna Graecia period and are typically Greek in their forms and patterns. Some of Calabria's most admired pottery and ceramics are from Trebisacce, Aspromonte, Bisignano, Gerace,

Hand-embroidered linen in Morano Calabro

Altomonte and Seminara. Trebisacce's historical connections with the Mycenaeans are evident in their massive earthenware jars used to store olive oil and grains, which now decorate Calabrian gardens. The ceramics from the hillside village of Seminara, settled by Byzantine monks, are treasured across the region for their bright colours and fruit reliefs decorating the enormous vases and urns, and the striking apotropaic masks used to ward off evil spirits.

Weaving, embroidery and silk

Weaving and embroidery can also be traced to Greek and Roman times. In Longobucco, the women produce exquisite handmade tapestries, particularly bedcovers, using the techniques and tools that have been employed for generations. Arab and Byzantine influences are evident in the decorative patterns and symbols that typify their designs. In the northern Albanian villages, blankets, tapestries, tablecloths and mats feature patterns and motifs that have been used since the 15th-century exodus from Albania. In San Giovanni in Fiore, the women embroider splendid textiles incorporating patterns and techniques from their Armenian heritage, while Tiriolo is famous for its delightful embroidered shawls called *vancali*. In the 15th century, Catanzaro was a sophisticated world producer of silk, linens and lace, and steps are currently being taken to revive the art of traditional weaving in the area.

Woodwork, wickerwork and metalwork

Metalwork is alive in San Giovanni in Fiore, where goldsmiths are still to be found, and in Dipignano and Serra San Bruno, where decorative wrought iron and copperware are produced. Woodworking is practised widely, and you'll find rustic kitchen utensils, including wooden spoons and bowls, in local markets. Lutes are still made in Delianuova and Bisignano. The traditional use of wicker and straw to produce rustic brooms, brushes and baskets is flourishing again in Soriano Calabro.

Cosenza province

Cosenza is one of Calabria's most compelling provinces, boasting a fascinating capital city with a complex history, two beautiful national parks in Pollino in the north and Sila in the east, a string of alluring seaside towns on its western shores, including Amantea, Paola and Diamante, and several enchanting hilltop towns, such as Altomonte and Morano Calabro.

On the west coast is the cobalt-coloured Tyrrhenian Sea, with its craggy coastline of cliffs and coves that is especially dramatic in the north, while to the east, on the calmer Ionian Sea, there are long, flat, sandy beaches.

Cosenza city

The provincial capital, Cosenza, is splendidly located, surrounded by lush mountains with fertile farmland, and sited at the confluence of two rivers. The Busento River separates Cosenza's *centro storico* from its modern town, while the Crati wends its way around the base of Pancrazio Hill, upon which the old city charmingly sprawls and spills down, somewhat overshadowed by its Castello Svevo (Swabian Castle).

The waterfront at Diamante on the western coast

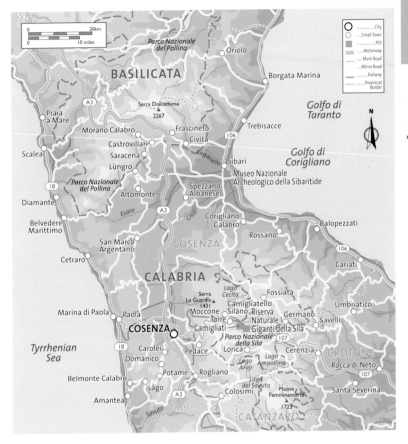

A city with a rich history and a freethinking and rebellious spirit, Cosenza has garnered mixed reviews over the years. The 17th-century chronicler Giuseppe Maria Galanti called it a Jewish ghetto without anything outstanding except its ancient name, while in the 18th century Giacomo Casanova saw it as a city with 'titled nobility, beautiful women and people not without education'.

It was revered as the 'Athens of Calabria' by 19th-century observer Davide Andreotti in *A History of the People of Cosenza* because of its accomplished town planning, splendid architecture, and complex layers of history and culture, while George Gissing wrote in his travelogue *By the Ionian Sea* (1901), 'To call the town picturesque is to use an inadequate word.'

The capital of Calabria's native people, the Bruttii or Bruttians, Cosentia was a Magna Graecia colony before being occupied by the Romans in 204 BC, after which it became an important stop on the Via Popilia linking the imperial capital to Reggio.

Fought over by the Arabs and Lombards, and then the Aragonese and Angevins – between whom the city continually shifted its loyalties – Cosenza was conquered, destroyed and rebuilt many times between the 13th and 15th centuries.

Despite great resistance, Cosenza was occupied by the Spanish in 1500, then the Austrians, who in turn were followed by the Bourbons. However, after being designated the seat of the Viceroy of Calabria, the city flourished culturally thanks to the establishment

Shopping and statues on Cosenza's Corso Mazzini

in 1511, on what is now Piazza XV Marzo, of the Accademia Cosentina, whose members included the revered humanist Aulo Gianni Parrasio, the philosopher Bernardino Telesio and the economist Antonio Serra.

With its vibrant intellectual life, discreet nobility, success from the silk trade and highly skilled artisans, Cosenza continued to prosper until the end of the 16th century. Under the French, however, the city was terribly suppressed and rebels were executed, leading to the creation of secret societies. Riots in 1821 and 1837 heralded the Risorgimento, followed by the historic uprising on 15 March 1844 that helped pave the way for Garibaldi's victory and the creation of an independent Kingdom of Italy.

These days, Cosenza is known as the 'Milan of Calabria'. An important commercial, industrial and agricultural centre for the region, it's home to Italy's youngest university, the University of Calabria, whose students ensure Cosenza has a more vibrant, youthful feel than other Calabrian cities.

In the modern part of town, the pedestrianised shopping street Corso Mazzini is lined with chic fashion boutiques and boasts a lively evening *passeggiata*. It also features a range of modern sculptures donated to Cosenza by the Italian-American art collector Carlo Bilotti, including *St George and the Dragon* by Salvador Dalí and *Hector and Andromache* by Giorgio de Chirico.

Some of Cosenza's *centro storico* steps can be steep

Across the river, the atmospheric cobblestone lanes of the hilly *centro storico* are where visitors spend most of their time. Grand government buildings, imposing theatres and elegant palazzi dominate the squares, while tall, dilapidated stone buildings tumble down the hillside, towering above skinny alleyways, washing strung between them.

Apart from those listed below, Cosenza's other highlights include the 10th-century Castello Svevo (Swabian Castle, *see p82*) and the 13th- to 15th-century Chiesa di San Francesco d'Assisi (Church of St Francis of Assisi, *see p83*).

Chiesa e Convento di San Domenico (Church and Convent of St Dominic)
Founded in 1448, the church has an austere exterior that hides a richly decorated, flamboyant white-and-gold interior hung with splendid paintings. The carved, painted organ dates from 1700.

The Gothic exterior of Cosenza's Duomo

Piazza Tommaso Campanella, off Via San Quattromani. Open: daily 9am–12.30pm & 4–8pm. Free admission.

Il Duomo (Cathedral)

The 11th-century cathedral was seriously damaged by the 1184 earthquake. Rebuilt in 1222, it was expanded and embellished in the 18th century when an enormous Baroque structure was erected around the old building, before being renovated again in the early 19th century and given a Gothic façade. Inside is the splendid tomb of Isabella of Aragon.
Piazza Duomo, Corso Telesio.
Open: daily 9am–12.30pm & 4–8pm. Free admission.

Piazza XV Marzo

This grand square is best appreciated at weekends, when it isn't in use as a car park for government workers. The central monument to the philosopher Bernardino Telesio is by sculptor Achille d'Orsi. Opposite the **Palazzo del Governo** (Government House, built 1844–7) is the elegant orange **Teatro Rendano,** and next door to this is the esteemed 16th-century **Accademia Cosentina,** home to one of southern Italy's richest libraries. Alongside the Palazzo del Governo is **Villa Vecchia**, a beautiful garden that was established in the 19th century.
Corso Telesio.

Buildings on Piazza Duomo

Walk: Cosenza

This is a climb around the cobblestone streets of Cosenza's hilly centro storico to explore its attractions, from Renaissance palazzi to remarkable churches and a robust castle. It's a part of the city that's very much lived in; children play in the alleys and old men sit and gossip outside their shops.

Allow two hours. Start on tiny Piazza Tommaso Campanella, off Via San Quattromani.

1 Chiesa e Convento di San Domenico (Church and Convent of St Dominic)

Take a look inside this important church and convent, which boasts an ornate interior (*see p79 & p81*).
Cross Ponte Martire, then cross the road to Corso Telesio.

2 Corso Telesio

Skinny Corso Telesio (formerly Via dei Mercanti) winds through the heart of the old town. There are still some endearingly old-fashioned shops with retro signs – and note the carpenters, antique restorers and blacksmiths.
Follow Corso Telesio to Piazza Duomo.

3 Duomo (Cathedral)

Admire the cathedral's austere exterior from the outside before heading in to appreciate the vastness of the interior, the rose windows, the important works of art, and the beautiful tomb of Isabella of Aragon (*see p81*).
Continue on to Piazza XV Marzo.

4 Piazza XV Marzo

Take in the elegant buildings on this grand square (*see p81*) and the important sculpture in the centre, and take a peek at the pretty garden, Villa Vecchia, established in the 19th century.
Take the steps beside Teatro Rendano, and pass the college building and Archi di Ciaccio. Turn right into Via dei Normanni.

5 Castello Svevo (Swabian Castle)

Foundations for this imposing castle were laid by the Saracens in the 11th century on the ruins of ancient Rocca Brutia. Frederick II added the octagonal tower in 1239, and the Angevins and Bourbons made further modifications.
Follow Via dei Normanni and turn right on to the path that zigzags down.

6 Convento delle Cappuccinelle (Capuchin Convent)

Another conservative exterior conceals an interior decorated with frescoes and beautiful paintings, including Pietro Negroni's *Immacolata* (1558).

Follow Corso Vittorio Emanuele II to Via Archi di Ciaccio, then turn left on Via Argento.

Continue past Piazza dei Follari, noting the bullet holes on the buildings from contemporary battles. Follow Via Padolisi then Via del Seggio to Piazza Berardi.

7 Chiesa e Convento di Santa Maria delle Vergini (Church and Convent of the Virgin Mary)

The decorative tuff exterior of this stunning building hides a beautiful carved wooden interior and paintings including Giovanni da Taranto's 13th-century *Madonna del Pilerio*.

8 Chiesa di San Francesco d'Assisi (Church of St Francis of Assisi)

In this church, founded by a disciple of the saint in 1217, can be seen Daniele Russo's impressive painting *Perdono d'Assisi* (1618). The church reopened in 2010 after a four-year renovation.

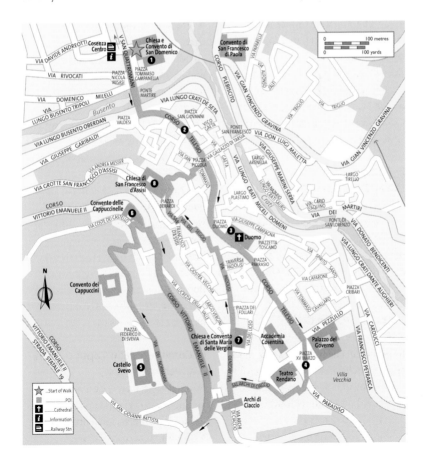

Amantea

One of Calabria's most enjoyable cities, Amantea has a lively modern centre and, hugging the cliffs of a rocky hill above it, one of the region's most alluring *centri storici*, accessed by wide marble staircases that hint at its aristocratic past.

Amantea has a fascinating history that reveals itself through the strength of character of its people. Bronze and Iron Age relics and other archaeological discoveries in the area, especially near the mouth of the Savuto River, suggest that Amantea was heavily settled by the Bruttii, Calabria's native people. A tribe of strapping warriors whose courage and endurance are legendary, the Bruttii are believed to have kept the Greeks at bay for decades.

Amantea's history as a city dates from the Romans, who established a

A shrine in Amantea's old town

large port there that really put the town on the map. After the Roman Empire's fall, the region was split between the Byzantines and Lombards, with the border passing Amantea – hence the imposing Byzantine castle that was built to protect the city. Not that this helped much against the Arabs, who captured Amantea in 839, making it an emirate or city-state. 'Amantea' is actually Arabic in origin, from Al Mantiah, meaning 'stronghold'. The Normans followed the Arabs and Byzantines, but historically it's the uprising by the people of Amantea against the Angevins in 1269 that's best remembered. Their reputation was cemented after their long resistance against Joseph Bonaparte's troops, who tried to capture their castle in 1806–7.

The ruins of Amantea's *castello* – known as 'La Rocca' because it sits atop the rock the *centro storico* clings to – are accessed by steep, narrow stairs and paths beginning near the Baroque cathedral or **Chiesa Matrice** (Mother Church), itself entered via a grand staircase. The Gothic **Chiesa di San Bernardino** (Church of St Bernard) dating from 1436 is also worth a look.

The *centro storico* is the best reason to visit Amantea and it's a delight to explore, with its elegant old pastel-coloured palazzi perched on the cliffs above the city, such as the grand 17th-century Palazzo Mirabelli and Palazzo delle Clarisse. The latter is now a restaurant with charming accommodation upstairs, and even if you're not staying it's possible to knock on the door and ask to see inside.

Amantea's small, modern commercial centre – like those in Reggio, Cosenza and Vibo Valentia, but unlike many elsewhere in Calabria – is a lovely place to spend some time, especially during a Sunday-afternoon *passeggiata* in the warmer months, when the main street and the waterfront promenade really come alive. As Amantea is by the sea, fishing has always been a mainstay of the economy here, and gastronomes will love the city's fantastic shops specialising in preserved treats, such as anchovies in different types of olive oil.

Belmonte Calabro

There is little to see or do at Belmonte Calabro, a beautiful hilltop village close to Amantea, from where you can see the city sprawled enchantingly across the hills. Yet its twisting alleyways, lined with a hotchpotch of medieval and modern architecture, are worth an hour's exploration in the early morning or late afternoon.

Cosenza's hilltop towns

Driving the back roads to Cosenza from Belmonte Calabro via Lago is a bit like travelling to the past in a time machine. Don't be surprised if you see old men carting firewood on the back of a mule accompanied by their elderly wives in long skirts and headscarves carrying axes. The people here lead simple lives.

Belmonte Calabro to Lago

The scenery is gorgeous. Crumbling stone houses are scattered across the hills, each seeming to possess a small vineyard. Lush green hills are smattered with birch forests, and sprinkled with vibrant wild flowers and flowering cactus bushes. Vines tangle themselves around tree trunks. There's the sound of birdsong, the sweet fragrance of honeysuckle, and lime-green lizards dart across the road. Lago itself is another lovely hilltop village.

Potame to Domanico

Potame sits splendidly on a small plateau. After Potame, a series of switchbacks takes you to slightly higher ground where you're likely to see birds of prey circling, signs for cows crossing (although no cows), snow in winter, and locals filling bottles from roadside natural spring fountains.

Domanico is a larger and more affluent village with smart stone houses, neatly tiled rooftops and a well-kept school. The older gentlemen wear suit jackets and hats and socialise in the small main square.

Carolei

The last interesting stop before the descent to Cosenza, Carolei is a large, attractive village that sprawls across a mountaintop. The doors of its grand old buildings open directly on to the street, and washing hangs from lines strung across the wrought-iron balconies.

Tyrrhenian coastal towns

Known as the Cedri Riviera (Citrus Coast), the northern Tyrrhenian coastline is an increasingly popular summer holiday destination for Italians. Outside the summer months, when traffic can be heavy and parking non-existent, all of the towns below can be visited in one day.

Paola

An important place of pilgrimage, tiny Paola is the birthplace of the nation's most admired saint, San Francesco di Paola (1416–1507). Born to parents who had prayed to St Francis of Assisi for a child, Francesco was cured of an eye affliction after spending time with the Franciscan monks and later entered the monastery.

After making a pilgrimage to Assisi with his parents, he went to live in seclusion and quiet prayer in a cave on the coast, later forming an order of hermit monks, the Minim Friars, who chose to live in great poverty. The patron saint of Calabria, as well as of boatmen and mariners, St Francis would famously sail to Sicily on his cloak and staff. He was revered as a prophet because he predicted the arrival of the Ottoman Turks, and his counsel was sought by kings.

While pilgrims make a beeline for his sanctuary, the **Santuario di San Francesco di Paola** (in a picturesque gully above the town), and for the birthplace of the saint, Paola is worth a wander simply for its charming

LA SANTINA AND OTHER SUPERSTITIONS

Some say they don't exist any more, while others argue that they never existed at all, but the *santina*, or psychic, was once a fixture of every Calabrian village. Blessed with the ability to 'see' and talk to the dead, and to perform miracles, *la santina* is still used to bless newborn animals. Still fervently believed in, however, is *malocchio* ('evil eye'), from the Italian for 'bad' (*male*) and 'eye' (*occhio*). With any form of illness there's always a sneaking suspicion that it is the symptom of a curse. Fortunately, there is always a *nonna* (grandma) around who can lift it, with either home remedies or incantations – for a small commission, of course!

atmosphere, attractive piazza and beautiful Baroque churches.

Belvedere Marittimo

After visiting the leafy modern town with its attractive marina and beach, drive up to the Baroque *centro storico* on the hill above town, built around and among the ruins of a Norman castle. Park your car near the pretty belvedere, lined with towering palm trees, then head up the steps and follow the dog-legged lane through the medieval entrance to explore this labyrinthine old town. Note elegant Palazzo Perez on your left.

Visit midweek or any day at midday and Belvedere Marittimo feels like a ghost town. Only the decorative ceramic reliefs on the buildings provide any kind of hint of the mayhem that can erupt on a midsummer weekend afternoon when the place is crammed with visitors to take in the atmosphere and buy some of the ceramics the town is famous for. There are panoramic views across the square and down to the coast from the 16th-century Chiesa Santa Maria del Popolo (Church of St Mary of the People).

Diamante

Diamante's grey-sand beach is not the most attractive, the paint on its dilapidated (albeit grand) pastel-coloured buildings is peeling, and the diminutive size of its old town leaves little room for development. Yet this northern Tyrrhenian seaside town has inexplicably become a rather fashionable destination among Italians in recent years.

If you're in the area, it's definitely worth parking your car (near the beach, as it's impossible to park in the *centro storico*) and taking a wander around the old town, where the buildings' walls are painted with murals. Try to visit on a weekend, when a market sprawls along the pleasant waterfront. Diamante is famous for its spicy peppers and sausages, and the stalls here sell delicious preserves in jars. Also popular with the locals is a van selling hot panini with spicy aniseed-tinged sausages, potatoes and mayonnaise.

Praia a Mare

One of the first Calabrian towns you'll come to if driving down the Tyrrhenian coast from Basilicata, Praia a Mare is a popular summer holiday spot. The

San Francesco di Paola is popular with pilgrims

main street is lined with eucalyptus trees and the seaside promenade with pine trees, yet the long, wide, grey-sand beach is rocky in parts and the concrete apartment buildings are rather shabby and in desperate need of a lick of paint. Still, there are canopied cafés on the waterfront, and sunbeds and umbrellas can be hired from the lidos, along with canoes, pedalos and sailing boats. Beach volleyball courts are set up on the sand, and go-karts are available for hire just across the road.

There is a smaller, more attractive, crescent-shaped beach south of the main one. It's rocky and a challenge to access, but it's more scenic, situated opposite a small, craggy island. There are several more attractive coves south of Praia towards Scalea, with crystal-clear waters that are wonderful for swimming, but Scalea itself is an even scruffier summer holiday resort.

Calabrian cuisine: some like it hot!

Every region of Italy has its own signature dishes or ingredients to give something like pasta a regional bent. Calabria has one of the most distinctive cuisines in the country, having over the centuries seen many waves of invaders and immigrants, including the Greeks, Romans, French, Arabs and Spaniards, all of whom have had remarkable influence on the region's food.

Local *peperoncini* (peppers)

While it's often described as *cucina povera* (peasant cooking), owing to the locals having to make the most of their often meagre raw materials, it's anything but unsophisticated. And the inventiveness born from the necessity of 'nose to tail' cooking (using all of a slaughtered animal), along with preserving, has made Calabria's hearty and spicy cuisine distinctive from those of neighbouring Sicily and regions to the north, while all the time remaining quintessentially Italian.

The main thing that sets Calabrian cuisine apart is the use of spices and herbs. Aniseed is used to flavour desserts and liqueurs. Capers preserved in brine or salt are staple ingredients. Fennel is used in cooking and to flavour sausages, as are black peppercorns. Chillies (red, green and yellow peppers) are eaten fresh, even chopped up and tossed into salads, while *peperoncini* (hot red crushed peppers) are ubiquitous, in everything from sausages to pasta, or simply spread on toast with olive oil. Every household has a good supply on hand.

While the sausages are hot, nothing quite compares to *'nduja*, a fiery pork sausage paste generally

Cipolla di Tropea – the famous, sweet red onions of Tropea

wonderful local olive oil. Even the roe from fish is preserved, and *bottarga* (dried tuna roe) is a speciality served as an appetiser or in pasta. Drying fish to preserve them is also popular, and you'll see *baccalà* (dried cod) on menus, often in pasta or as part of a salad.

The slaughtering of a pig is traditionally a big occasion in Calabria, where, until recently, famine was a constant companion. As a result, what can't be eaten is preserved, made either into sausages or into types of hams. Along with the usual cuts, *soppressata* (a dry-cured pork sausage) is a speciality, as is the Calabrian version of *guanciale*, made from cured pork cheek and pepper. It's traditionally used in pasta dishes.

spread on toasted bread with a drizzle of olive oil; it's not for those who don't like it hot! It's also used in pasta sauces and spread on pizzas, but it's used sparingly – a little of it goes a long way.

Thanks to Calabria's coastline, fish fresh from the sea, typically swordfish (*spada*) and tuna (*tonno*), dominate plates in the region. Whether it's *carpaccio*, preserved in jars, tossed in pasta or simply grilled, fish is on almost every menu. Anchovies also feature, often used from jars where they've been preserved in the

Melanzane (aubergines or eggplants) are omnipresent – grilled, preserved and stuffed – and are a feature on nearly every menu. In Vibo Valentia, the famous, sweet red Tropea onions are also everywhere (*see p60*). Legumes such as beans and chickpeas are used for hearty soups and pastas.

Calabrian desserts feature local figs and chestnuts. Fried pastries and baked biscotti-style biscuits abound, such as *'nzudda*, while liquorice is another top Calabrian export (*see p98*).

Morano Calabro

Calabrians will tell you that if you like Altomonte, you'll love Morano Calabro. Quite possibly one of the region's most enchanting towns, it is the view as you drive in (and also from the belvedere on the outskirts) of Morano Calabro spilling down the hillside – its ramshackle stone buildings seemingly stacked upon each other – that is so mesmerising. Many compare the marvellous sight to one of M C Escher's magical lithographs and woodcuts from his Italian period. Indeed, the artist spent time in Calabria in the early 1930s.

While close to the Pollino National Park, it's nevertheless well off the tourist circuit, and it is Morano's apparent lack of interest in attracting

The cobbled streets of Morano Calabro

visitors that makes it so appealing. At the time of writing there was only one hotel in town, several good restaurants and a handful of shops, and it's this absence of modernity that makes the medieval town so wonderful to explore. Climb the meandering alleys and stone stairways of the well-preserved town (stopping occasionally to enjoy the views) and you'll come across locals momentarily flabbergasted and then delighted to see foreigners exploring the steep streets. Little is signposted, but getting lost is half the fun.

Don't miss the **Chiesa di Santi Pietro e Paolo** (Church of Sts Peter and Paul) – boasting four beautiful statues by Pietro Bernini – at the top of the town near the ruined fortress and lovely grass belvedere, nor the 15th-century **Chiesa di San Bernardino** (Church of St Bernard) in Via Bernardino in the lower part of town.

It is worth timing your stay to coincide with a lively local festival, such as the medieval Festa della Bandiera (Festival of the Flag, see p18), which centres around two days of processions by a band and men on horseback through the decorated town. Much flag-waving is followed by eating, drinking and fireworks.

Altomonte

This beautifully preserved village of stone houses that crawl across a lush hilltop and spill down the mountain slopes is hailed as 'Calabria's Spoleto', a reputation enhanced by Altomonte's

The hilltop village of Altomonte

healthy calendar of gastronomic and music festivals.

Park at the bottom of the *centro storico*, as it's resident-only parking in the centre, and hike up the narrow cobblestone streets to take in the charming atmosphere. Most of the main attractions – there are only a few – are around the central square, along with spectacular views of the rooftops of the village and the surrounding fertile valley, which is becoming an important centre for *agriturismo*. The olive oil and wine from here are award-winning and among Italy's best.

The highlight of Altomonte is without a doubt its splendid 14th-century **Chiesa di Santa Maria della Consolazione** (Church of Our Lady of Consolation) on the main piazza.

Dating from the Angevin period, the church boasts beautiful French Gothic features. The interior is partly Baroque and contains some fine sculptures and paintings, including works by the 14th-century artists Simone Martini and Bernardo Daddi. That Altomonte is a town of aristocrats is evident by the elaborate tombs inside the church. On the far left aisle you'll notice the impressive tomb of the nobleman Filippo Sangineto, along with the tombs of the Ruffo family and monuments belonging to the Sanseverino family.

Don't miss the pretty cloisters of the former monastery adjoining the church, now belonging to the local municipality, and the magnificent mountain vistas from the courtyard behind the church.

Castrovillari

Like a pointed finger, the picturesque city of Castrovillari, some 75km (47 miles) north of Cosenza, is perched dramatically on a hilltop jutting out into the farming valley below. Like its neighbour Morano Calabro, Castrovillari also makes a good base for excursions into the rugged Pollino National Park nearby.

Once hailed as a foodie destination after the restaurant La Locanda di Alia was included in the Michelin guide, Castrovillari has seen its gastronomic reputation diminished in recent years with Alia's decline and the fact that no other great restaurants have followed in its wake. Indeed, Morano Calabro could take up the mantle in the future, with its excellent restaurant or three, and being a much more enjoyable place to stay. Castrovillari unfortunately suffers from horrific traffic, a baffling one-way road system that frustrates visitors, and a dreadful lack of parking.

A pleasant modern town and a few historical sights nevertheless make it an interesting place to while away an hour. Situated at the tip of Castrovillari's pointed finger, the compact old town is home to the ruins of a 15th-century

Castrovillari rises out of the valley below it

Aragonese castle and, opposite, the
Chiesa di Santa Maria del Castello
(Church of St Mary of the Castle).

Ignore any suggestions to see the
archaeological 'museum' nearby, which
looks more like an exhibition hastily
slapped together by high-school
students, and instead enjoy the cloisters
of the building it resides in, the
Convento di San Francesco d'Assisi
(Convent of St Francis of Assisi, *Via San
Francesco*), founded in 1220. The present
building dates from 1809, when the
convent was transformed into a military
hospital. The streets in this surrounding
area are rather atmospheric, too.

Parco Nazionale del Pollino
(Pollino National Park)

Straddling the border of the regions of
Basilicata and Calabria, and taking its
name from the Pollino Massif (highest
peak 2,267m/7,438ft), Pollino National
Park at 1,820sq km (700sq miles) is
Italy's largest protected area, established
in 1992.

The southern parts of the park, south
of the A3, are more akin to a wilderness
area, wild and wonderfully lacking in
infrastructure, compared to the northern
section in Basilicata, which is dotted with
villages. While Pollino is becoming
increasingly popular as a hiking
destination, the lack of mapped and
signposted trails makes it challenging for
all but the most experienced hikers to
explore without a guide, but it's easy
enough to organise a guide through
hotels and tourist offices in the region.

A wild verbascum in Pollino

The park's greatest appeal is its
wealth of landscapes, including the vast
areas of impenetrable wilderness at its
centre, the fertile valleys and rolling
hills on the park's edge, the striking
deep valley gorges, and the many
rivers and streams that run through
the park, such as the Coscile, Lao,
Sinni and Raganello.

Pollino is home to an array of
wildlife, too, including the Italian wolf,
roe deer and European otter, and
impressive birdlife, particularly birds of
prey such as the peregrine falcon, red
kite, lanner falcon, Egyptian vulture,
golden eagle and black woodpecker.
The park's symbol is the Bosnian pine,
and Pollino is one of the few areas in
which it still grows in Italy.

Civita

Prepare to find somewhere to pull the car over on your approach into Civita. The views of the small village of stone houses, strung across a ridge beneath a rock of a mountain beside the Raganello Gorge, are simply breathtaking.

The compact, well-preserved village itself is also a joy to explore. The main square, Piazza Municipio, is flanked by stone houses and a few elegant palazzi and, on your right as you enter the square, the Museo Etnico Arbëresh (Ethnic Museum of Albanian Culture, *see opposite*). The 17th-century **Chiesa di Santa Maria Assunta** (Church of Our Lady of the Assumption) with its splendid gold mosaics and icons is also worth a look, as is the **Ponte del Diavolo** (Devil's Bridge) just outside the village. If you miss the sign, ask the locals to steer you in the right direction.

A local produce shop in Civita

IT'S ALL GREEK TO ME

The long and colourful history of Calabria has left its mark with a myriad of languages and dialects still being spoken – despite standard Italian being the official language since the late 1800s. In the north of the region, the language often spoken is a dialect of Neapolitan called Cosentino. In the south, you might hear dialects of the Sicilian language, collectively known as Southern Calabro. Albanians who settled centuries ago still speak in the Arbëresh dialect of the Albanian language, while Griko (a modern Greek dialect) is spoken by people in the Magna Graecia region. Some Calabrian dialects even have some French and Spanish influence. Don't worry, *Buon giorno* will still elicit a response!

On the edge of Pollino National Park, and 12km (7½ miles) from Castrovillari, Civita is ideally placed for exploring the national park, and indeed was planting the seeds for the development of a small *agriturismo* industry at the time of writing. A number of bed and breakfasts are set to open in Civita's atmospheric *centro storico* and around the surrounding valley. Being so close to Pollino, the village makes a great base for hikers, and, indeed, guides can be arranged in the village. Ask at the tourist office (erratic hours) or shops on the main square.

Civita is one of 34 villages in Calabria of Albanian heritage, working hard to maintain their traditions, practise their unique customs and speak their own language. There are bilingual signs here and in other towns such as Frascineto, Spezzano Albanese and Lungro (the spiritual centre of Albanians in Calabria since the 15th century, although of less interest to tourists).

Museo Etnico Arbëresh (Ethnic Museum of Albanian Culture)

Run by the Gennaro Placco Cultural Association (which seems to consist of members of one family), this tiny two-storey museum documents the history of Albanian migrations to Calabria since the 1400s through a fascinating exhibition of everyday items, household implements, farming tools, a loom, handicrafts, costumes, historical records and photographs. It's not the most professional display and appears to be haphazardly organised, yet it's intriguing, the staff are friendly, and the small insight it provides into Albanian culture in Calabria makes it easily worth half an hour of your time.

Piazza Municipio. Tel: (0981) 730 1933.
www.museoetnicoarberesh.it.
Open: Mar–Sept daily 10am–12.30pm &
4–8pm; other times by appointment.
Admission charge.

Sibari (Sybaris)

Sybaris was the first Greek colony in Magna Graecia and one of its most prosperous, and its citizens were thought to have enjoyed a higher quality of life than those of other cities. The excavations at the site of ancient Sybaris and Roman Thurium compose one of the world's largest archaeological sites (1,000ha/2,470 acres; Pompeii's site measures 50ha/124 acres), and reveal a Greek city of over 100,000 people who were generally happy, healthy and wealthy. This is suggested by the riches discovered at the site, including a wealth of gold jewellery and sophisticated inventions such as a

The ancient ruins of Sybaris

chamber pot and pasta-maker, and written laws that ensured quiet, shady streets, guaranteed by a ban on noisy traders, and a tree-planting programme.

While the ruins at the site include a Roman *decumanus* (main street), Roman baths and a villa with mosaics, unfortunately for anyone other than

The atmospheric old town of Rossano

archaeologists, there is little in the way of impressive structures of the kind you see in Sicily, and you'll get more out of the museum itself, from where you can see the site, both in the distance and in model form.

The archaeological park is off the SS106, 4km (2½ miles) from the museum. Look for the sign 'Scavi di Sybari'. While it should theoretically be possible to visit at any time, the gates are often locked. Free admission.

Museo Nazionale Archeologico della Sibaritide (National Museum of Sybaritic Archaeology)

Situated in a striking modern white building, the National Museum of Sybaritic Archaeology makes up for what the archaeological park lacks with an outstanding collection of finds from the nearby excavations.

Highlights include Bronze Age pottery and ceramics from the 17th to 14th centuries BC, finds from a tomb from around 330 AC (After Christ, as Italian archaeologists say), including a bronze warrior's helmet, and one of the museum's most impressive relics, that of a Greek statue of a bull charging, restored by the Romans and dating from the 4th to 5th centuries AC. This was the last significant find in 2004, before the dig ran out of funding.

Casa Bianca, Sibari, Route 534, off the SS106. Tel: (0981) 793 91.
Open: Tue–Sun 9am–7.30pm.
Admission charge.

Sibari's museum

Rossano

The elegant, aristocratic old hilltop town of Rossano is an absolute gem. Just 12km (7½ miles) inland from the drab modern town of Rossano Scalo, Rossano's *centro storico* is worlds away in atmosphere. However, while Rossano's streets are lined with grand public buildings and sumptuous palazzi, it's very much a working-class town now. The offices of the Communist Party and unions lie off the main squares, Piazza Steri and Piazza Martucci, where the elderly gentlemen of the town like to sit and watch the world go by.

Apart from those listed below, Rossano's highlights include the splendid **Chiesa e Monastero di Santa Maria Nuova Odigitria** (Church and Monastery of St Mary), founded in 1090, the imposing remains of **Il Castello di San Angelo** (St Angel's Castle), dating from 1543, and the Byzantine **L'Oratorio di San Marco** (St Mark's Oratory), built between the 9th and 10th centuries and similar in style to La Cattolica in Stilo (*see pp50–51*).

As you explore the hilly streets, look out for the following palazzi: the enormous Palazzo Martucci, the pretty Palazzo Amarelli (boasting sky-blue shutters and owned by the liquorice-making family), the lovely lemon-and-

LIQUORICE MEMENTOS

Calabria is one of the world's best sources of liquorice, with the plant growing naturally all over the area. This black, bittersweet delight, made for centuries in the region by Amarelli, is now created with a mix of old-fashioned insider knowledge and computer-assisted processing, but the taste remains as pure as ever. At the Amarelli headquarters there is a gift shop where you can buy the original liquorice lozenges, but the company has branched out, and you can now also buy liquorice-flavoured grappa (an acquired taste), chocolate (mmmm!) and pasta (not so much). Thankfully, the pure liquorice made by Amarelli is still sold in those delightful retro tins seen all over Italy and exported throughout the world, which make great souvenirs.

Inside the Amarelli Liquorice Factory museum

white Palazzo Sorrentino and the imposing Palazzo de Rosis. Many feature magnificently decorated portals, elaborately carved coats of arms and elegant wrought-iron balconies.

Amarelli Fabbrica di Liquirizia (Amarelli Liquorice Factory)

The longest-operating and finest liquorice producers in the world, the Amarelli family began extracting sap from the liquorice root (*Glycyrrhiza glabra*) as far back as 1731. An important and influential aristocratic family (one Amarelli was a crusader, another was a politician, another founded Messina University), the Amarellis still operate the factory and, across the road, the fascinating museum (and gift shop) dedicated to the delicious art and situated in the splendid 15th-century Amarelli residence. You can join guided visits (in Italian, English, German and French) of the museum throughout the day, and factory tours are held at 10am and 11am.

Litorale di Rossano, SS106.
Tel: (0983) 511 219. www.liquirizia.it.
Open: daily 10am–7pm. Free admission.

Duomo (Cathedral)

Awkwardly positioned below a narrow path that zigzags down the hill from the main piazza, Rossano's Baroque cathedral is difficult to appreciate fully from above – all but its bell tower's splendid majolica-tiled dome, that is, which is perfectly situated for late-afternoon photographs. While the original cathedral dated from the 11th century, the current structure was built following the 1836 earthquake.

Rossano's clock tower

The cathedral has a beautiful, ornate interior boasting a grand organ (1622), exquisite mosaic tiles near the altar, and a wealth of important sacred art. The highlight is the *Madonna Achiropita*, a much-venerated 9th-century Byzantine fresco believed to have been painted by angels – its Greek epithet translates as 'not painted by hand'.

Piazza Duomo. Tel: (0983) 521 875.
Open: daily 9.30am–12.30pm &
4.30–8.30pm. Free admission.

Museo Diocesano (Diocesan Museum)

Rossano was an important Byzantine centre between the 8th and 11th centuries, and, in addition to exhibiting sacred relics from this and other historical periods, the museum is home to *Il Codex Purpureus* (*The Purple Codex*), a beautiful illuminated manuscript illustrating the life of Christ on parchment. It was brought to Rossano by monks fleeing Palestine, and despite being enclosed in a cabinet under lock and key – you'll have to ask to see it – the precious manuscript has faded considerably and is no longer the reddish-purple colour it was said to be. The page it's opened on is worth a look, however, and there's a laminated colour photocopy as well.

Piazza Duomo. Tel: (0983) 525 263.
Open: Jul–mid-Sept daily 9am–1pm &
4.30–8pm; mid-Sept–Jun Tue–Sun
9.30am–12.30pm & 4–7pm.
Admission charge.

The Grand Tour in Calabria

From the 18th century onwards, intrepid and usually privileged travellers set off from England, and later America, on the Grand Tour. Their aim was to discover Europe, and Italy in particular, and by doing so to educate themselves – through language, archaeology, painting, music and literature – in the art of knowing, of being cosmopolitan.

Most travellers stopped at Naples, with only the more adventurous continuing by sea as far afield as Sicily, skipping Calabria on account of its poor road network and roving bandits. English writer Norman Douglas (1868–1952), however, was one of the brave travellers who spent a considerable amount of time in Calabria, journeying the length and breadth of the region in 1907, 1911 and again in 1937, observing and interviewing, and reflecting as he went, and maintaining scrupulously detailed travel diaries.

Calabria, after all, was a perfect destination for Grand Tourists. The region once belonged to the mighty Magna Graecia civilisation and had a long association with the ancient Greeks and Romans; it was rich in archaeological treasures and dotted with exquisite Byzantine churches, Carthusian monasteries, abbeys and cathedrals, which hid a wealth of vibrant frescoes, illuminated manuscripts and important paintings.

In addition, Calabria boasted an array of landscapes of the kind the Grand Tourists, romantics at heart, found so alluring, from craggy coves and creamy beaches to wooden forests and dramatic valleys, along with mysterious mountain-top villages, home to mystical religions and secret societies, which the Tourists' insatiable curiosity propelled them to explore.

A typical Grand Tourist, Douglas fell in love with the untamed nature of Calabria, its complex layers of history, its unspoilt natural beauty, its proud people and their intriguing customs. He wrote: 'It was exhilarating to traverse these middle heights with their aerial views over the Ionian and down olive-covered hill-sides towards the wide valley of the Crati and the lofty Pollino range, now swimming in the midsummer haze.'

Douglas's book *Old Calabria* (1915) is probably the most comprehensive narrative ever written about the region. Other travellers who explored

Torre Camigliati, an 18th-century hunting lodge in Camigliatello Silano

the area include Henry Swinburne, Alexandre Dumas, Edward Lear and George Gissing.

Parco Old Calabria at Torre Camigliati

As part of a larger project to revive 'Grand Tour' tourism in Calabria and other parts of southern Italy, 17 wild parks, gardens and other places have been dedicated as Parchi Letterari (Literary Parks). These are atmospheric locations encountered by great authors and poets, from Giuseppe Tomasi di Lampedusa to Luigi Pirandello, who were so inspired by them that they created literary works that immortalised the places.

The leafy parkland of Torre Camigliati, the grand ancestral home of the noble Barracco family, is one such Parco Letterario. What does this actually mean? It means that you can wander the beautiful grounds to your heart's content, inhale the aromatic air, and stop to smell the wild flowers, preferably with a sketchbook, a book of poetry or a copy of Norman Douglas's *Old Calabria*, available for sale at the gift shop in the cultural centre at the former baronial residence. There's also a library, multimedia centre and a photo exhibition inside illustrating the Calabrian Grand Tour. To take full advantage of the delightful idea, check in to Torre Camigliati for a couple of nights, then grab a copy of their *Calabrian Grand Tour Itinerary* and set off on your own adventure (*see p169*). *Torre Camigliati, Parco Old Calabria, Camigliatello Silano. Tel: (0984) 578 200. www.oldcalabria.it. Call ahead. Free admission.*

View across the Sila National Park

Camigliatello Silano

The delightful alpine-like village of Camigliatello Silano is a short drive from Cosenza (around 30km/19 miles) and is the best base for exploring the beautiful lakes and thick forests of the Sila National Park.

If the former baronial residence Torre Camigliati (see p101) isn't reason enough to visit, then the gastronomic delights (smoked cheeses, cold cuts, preserves, Calabrian wine and porcini mushrooms when in season) cramming the shelves at the many mouth-watering shops lining Camigliatello's main street should prove a further enticement. If any additional evidence of Camigliatello's gastronomic credentials were needed, the town plays host to a number of gourmet food festivals and is home to one of Calabria's finest restaurants, La Tavernetta (see p169).

Fill a picnic basket with some treats before setting off for a lakeside drive (see pp106–7), or a backpack before heading off for a hike or horse riding, biking, canoeing, boating, fishing or – in winter – skiing and snowboarding. The Pro Loco office (see p169) or hotel can put you in touch with professional guides for hiking, horse-riding or biking excursions through the park.

Hiking is one of the most popular park activities and a small booklet, *A Piedi in Sila Grande* (Italian only), available from Pro Loco offices, sets out detailed itineraries for walking and hiking in the park. Hikes begin, for example, from Camigliatello at Torre Camigliati (an hour to Croce di Magara), at Cecita (an hour and a half to Serra La Vulga at 1,298m/4,259ft), at Moccone (an hour and a half to Serra La Guardia) and at Fossiata (an hour and a half to Macchialonga at 1,311m/4,301ft).

Campi da Ski

A few kilometres from town, this simple ski complex offers basic winter-sports facilities, including a small but steep ski slope, half a dozen ski schools and a fully enclosed modern chairlift, and you can rent ski equipment from the wooden cabins in the car park. It can't compete with northern Italy's ski centres, but a couple of hours here can be fun. The drawcards are the beautiful setting and proximity to Camigliatello.

La Nave della Sila (The Ship of Sila)

Stunningly set in a beautifully renovated barn, Camigliatello's main cultural attraction is this superb museum of emigration. Through the innovative use of striking graphics, photographs and atmospheric audio and video, the fascinating exhibition charts the mass emigration of Calabrians to the USA, Australia,

Canada and Brazil. An interactive kiosk allows visitors to explore their family histories, and there's a library and café. Explanations are currently in Italian only, but the visuals are so illuminating that non-Italian speakers will still enjoy the display.

Torre Camigliati, Camigliatello Silano, near Parco Old Calabria.
Tel: (081) 667 599 or email: info@ oldcalabria.org to make a booking.

Parco Nazionale della Sila (Sila National Park)

This park is the green heart of the Cosenza region, renowned for its immense forested mountain ranges, abundant wildlife, and still, blue lakes that sparkle like diamonds. The Parco

Camigliatello Silano's canopy of trees

Cosenza province

Nazionale della Sila, often called just La Sila, actually consists of three areas: the Sila Grande (the area covered by the drive on *pp106–7*), Sila Piccola (straddling the border with Crotone) and Sila Greca in the north, an Albanian area since the immigration of the 1500s.

The most scenic landscapes – glassy lakes skirted by sandy beaches, healthy horses grazing on lush, green meadows, thick forests of fir and pine – are in Sila Grande, but everywhere you go there is the all-pervading fragrance of honey-scented wild flowers and fresh air. Deep in the coniferous forests, the pristine habitat plays host to some of Calabria's most diverse wildlife, including deer, wolves, wild boar, and birds ranging from woodpeckers and eagle owls to splendid peregrine falcons.

The lakes

The countryside around the still, turquoise **Lago Arvo** is idyllic, with

Beautiful horses in the national park

green, rolling hills, dense woodlands and towering fir trees, and in spring you'll find fields positively blanketed in wild flowers. Lorica is a lovely, laid-back village of holiday houses overlooking the lake. A *passeggiata panoramica* skirts the water where strategically placed benches allow you to sit and relax and enjoy the picturesque scenery.

Somewhat smaller than Lago Arvo, **Lago Ampollino** is surrounded by thick pine forests and boasts narrow, sandy beaches. The main difference lies in the mood set by the accommodation on its shores. With its campsite and holiday flats, Lago Ampollino attracts families here for fishing, swimming and boating, whereas Lago Arvo, with its holiday houses and hotel, draws more laid-back couples. Not far away, **Lago del Savuto** is smaller and less attractive, but completists may want to check it out.

The countryside surrounding **Lago Cecita** is as idyllic as that around the other lakes, with kilometres of log fences on either side of the road, endless fields of wild flowers, and some of the tallest and oldest trees you'll see in Calabria. However, on the shores of the lake, the forest is less dense and there is more cleared farmland, giving Cecita a different feel from the others.

Riserva Naturale I Giganti della Sila (The Giants of Sila Natural Reserve)
You can wander under the spooky dark canopy of Calabria's tallest and oldest trees just out of Camigliatello, along a potholed road (muddy after winter), near Croce di Magara. Thought to be 'ancient' species, the pine trees here are said to be over 350 years old and around 40m (130ft) high.
Signposted, it's 3km (1¾ miles) off the Cosenza–Crotone road and a ten-minute walk from the car park.

Lago Ampollino in Sila National Park

Drive: Parco Nazionale della Sila

This gentle drive, beginning in Cosenza and ending in Camigliatello Silano, snakes through the national park's most scenic landscapes. The roads through the Sila are narrow and winding, yet they are less challenging than those in the Aspromonte and Serra San Bruno. While the distances aren't great, the continual meandering means it's slow going.

Allow five or six hours for stops to explore and enjoy lunch.

Start at the base of Cosenza's centro storico and take Lungo Crati della Pietà adjacent to the Crati River. Follow the signs for Pedace.

1 Pedace

At this charming village, stop on the main piazza, where old men doze, and admire the stone **Chiesa SS Apostoli Pietro e Paolo** (Church of Sts Peter and Paul). The beautifully restored interior features elaborately decorated chapels, exquisitely painted ceilings and a pretty blue cupola. Note the separate bell tower outside.

Follow the signs to Pietrafitta and Aprigliano. Just out of Pedace, stop to savour the vistas of the hilltop town. Once through Aprigliano, follow the signs for San Giovanni in Fiore. You'll soon arrive at the signposted Sila National Park. At the first intersection, turn left.

2 Lago Arvo and Lorica

Take in the idyllic countryside around the glassy lake (*see p104*). Once at Lorica, take a stroll along the *passeggiata panoramica* skirting the lake and take in the tranquil scene from the well-placed benches.

Follow 'lungo di lago' signs for the lakeside drive. At the town of Rovale, follow the San Giovanni in Fiore signs. Or turn right to continue to explore Lago Arvo, returning to this junction when you're finished. At the next T-junction, turn right to visit Lago Ampollino.

3 Lago Ampollino

Lago Ampollino (*see p104*) is surrounded by thick pine forests and skirted by beaches, so you can kick about on the sand or hire a boat for a row on the lake.

At the lake's end, turn around, head back across the bridge over the dam walls and follow the signs to San Giovanni in Fiore.

4 San Giovanni in Fiore

San Giovanni in Fiore's dreadful traffic, confusing layout and bad signage can

be offputting. Most travellers drive straight through, but, if you can park, the town better reveals itself on a stroll around the *centro storico*.
Follow the signs for Germano, then for Fossiata, then Camigliatello.

5 Lago Cecita

Kilometres of log fences greet your approach to this lake (*see p105*).
Continue to follow the Camigliatello signs. As you approach town, turn left at the sign for Parco Old Calabria at Torre Camigliati. Stop at La Nave della Sila.

6 La Nave della Sila (The Ship of Sila)

Visit this superb museum to gain an appreciation of the extent of the mass

emigration from Calabria (*see p103*).
Continue on this road to Parco Old Calabria at Torre Camigliati.

7 Parco Old Calabria at Torre Camigliati

Make like a 'Grand Tourist' as Norman Douglas did (*see pp100–101*) and mosey around the wild gardens at this wonderful literary park.
Return to the main road and turn left for Camigliatello.

8 Camigliatello Silano

Pick up some delicious treats from the mouthwatering shops in this lovely town (*see p102*).
Head back to Cosenza or check into one of Camigliatello's charming hotels.

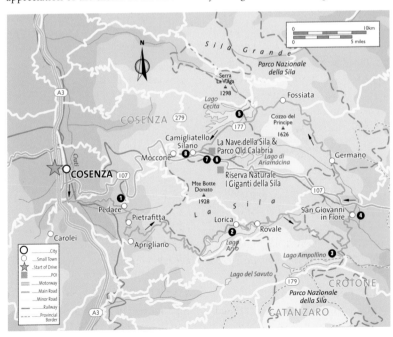

The Mezzogiorno

Mezzogiorno literally means 'midday', the hottest part of the day and the time when Italians stop whatever they're doing for a few hours to slowly savour a meal, often with family or friends. They take some time out to let their food digest and will probably have a nap, rejuvenating themselves for the rest of the day's work and other activities.

The fierce heat being a dominant characteristic of Italy's south, Mezzogiorno is also the name given to the somnolent, sun-drenched southern regions of Abruzzi, Puglia, Basilicata, Campania, Molise, Sardinia, Sicily and Calabria. It's apt, considering that this is a part of Italy known for its year-round sunshine, fertile (for the most part) land, slower

Mezzogiorno is all about enjoying a meal in a pleasant climate

pace of life and easy-going attitude. It's typically Mediterranean in many ways. Not coincidentally, these regions historically came under the control of the Kingdom of Sicily.

The term Mezzogiorno was first used in reference to southern Italy in the 18th century and was later popularised when it was adopted by the political and military leader Giuseppe Garibaldi (1807–82), who dedicated his life to the struggle for liberation of Italy from Austrian dominance. The unification of Italy wouldn't have been possible without Garibaldi, and he was a great hero to the Italians, especially the peoples of the south.

Garibaldi had a special interest in the plight of the southern Italians, most of whom were poverty-stricken, illiterate and inclined to a bit of banditry to improve their lot in life. Garibaldi had an ability to inspire like no other Italian leader had before, and he used his passion for the impoverished Mezzogiorno to call the men of the south to arms.

Economically, socially and spiritually depleted after the centuries of occupation and plundering, especially by the Spanish, the southern peoples

Peaches growing on the Sibari plain – agriculture has always been important in Calabria

united in their destitution as much as in their shared weather patterns, habits and customs. A typical question when one person met another was not 'How are you?' but 'What did you eat today?' (*Che si mangiato oggi?*), or, worse, 'Did you eat today?' (*Ha mangiato oggi?*).

Even after Italy's unification in 1860, and following the industrialisation of northern Italy, the south remained poor and underdeveloped, and the increasingly prosperous northern Italians started to look down upon the lower underclasses of the south. As a result, the southern Italians became increasingly united – against the north.

Although half of the land in the south was arid and non-arable (the rest was fortunately rich and fertile), agriculture remained the mainstay of the economy. The people looked to each other and the bonds they had forged to find ways out of their poverty and means by which to survive. In the early 20th century,

southerners started leaving Italy in droves, and under the Fascists the situation deteriorated even further, the economy plummeted and disease spread. In their new homes in Australia and North and South America, the bonds of family and friends from the Mezzogiorno would help the emigrants survive and succeed.

It was during this period, with the rise in power and notoriety of the Calabrian and Sicilian Mafias, that the meaning of Mezzogiorno took on even more negative connotations and suggested a connection to a place that wasn't only illiterate and poverty-stricken but also mired in crime.

It's only been in the last decade or so, with the government crackdown on the Mafia and crime and the rise of tourism in the south, that Mezzogiorno has come to suggest a more relaxed and enviable kind of lifestyle in a warmer climate, and one focused on appreciating the simplest pleasures in life: sunshine and food.

Crotone province

The compact province of Crotone extends from the end of the instep to the beginning of the ball of Italy's boot, from Cirò Marina, Calabria's celebrated wine-growing region on the province's northeast coast, to the peninsula of Capo Rizzuto, which juts out into the cobalt-coloured Ionian Sea in the south. There, Capo Colonna, the last surviving column from the Temple of Hera, stands alone, and nearby the spectacular Aragonese Castle appears to float at sea.

One of Magna Graecia's most important cities, ancient Kroton was founded in 710 BC by the Achaean colonist Myscellus. Renowned for its sunny climate, fertile land and superb medical schools, it gave birth to generations of victorious Olympic athletes such as the wrestling champion Milo. The city's other famous residents included philosopher-mathematician Pythagoras, who lived here around 530 BC, and the great Carthaginian military commander Hannibal (216 BC). The city's decline began in 480 BC, when it fell first to Locri, then to the Carthaginians, Romans, Ostrogoths, Saracens and Normans.

Crotone

A small, laid-back port city with an attractive *lungomare* (waterfront promenade) and sandy beaches, Crotone's tiny old quarter with its narrow alleyways is a fascinating place to while away a few hours exploring its impressive castle, engaging archaeological museum and myriad churches and palazzi lining the streets. Most of the buildings of the *centro storico* are dilapidated with peeling paint and window shutters bolted closed, giving it a ramshackle charm.

Architecturally a mishmash owing to the many times it has been rebuilt following earthquakes, Crotone's commercial centre nevertheless has a certain elegance, most evident in the lovely arcades of the streets running off Piazza Pitagora. Many of the graceful buildings stretching from here along Via Poggioreale to the seafront have been renovated, although, just a block or two behind, the backstreet tenements are covered in graffiti. There is a bustling fresh food market in the mornings between Via Poggioreale and Corso Vittorio Emanuele.

The seafront is the place to be, however, especially during the summer months. At weekends, locals cram the outside tables at the cafés and bars, and in the balmy evenings everyone in town

seems to be out jogging, power-walking, strolling or lining up at the pizzerie and *gelaterie*.

Castello Carlo V (Castle of Charles V)
With its massive moat, enormous walls and imposing bastions, this formidable castle is one of southern Italy's most impressive fortresses. Like the rest of the city's architecture, it's a hotchpotch of styles, its foundations from the 9th century, with further structures dating from the 15th, 16th and 17th centuries.

Its **Museo Civico** hosts interesting temporary exhibitions.
Piazza Castello. Tel: castle (0962) 921 231, museum (0962) 921 232. Open: Tue–Sat 9am–1pm & 3–6.50pm, Sun 9am–12.30pm. Free admission (charge for special exhibitions).

Museo Archeologico Nazionale (National Archaeology Museum)
This superb museum may be small, but it has a superlative collection of Bronze (Cont. on p116)

Walk: Crotone's *centro storico*

This stroll within the old city's 16th-century walls takes you to the key sights by way of Crotone's elegant old palazzi, once the residences of noble families, now in varying states of disrepair, their façades peeling and their windows boarded.

Allow one to two hours, including visits to the museums and castle.

Start at the centro storico entrance on Corso Vittorio Emanuele, with Piazza Duomo directly in front, then turn right and walk to Chiesa dell'Immacolata.

1 Chiesa dell'Immacolata (Church of the Immaculate Conception)

This pretty yellow-and-white 18th-century church was built on the ruins of a 16th-century church. The attractive neoclassical façade features eight columns and two niches holding statues, while inside there's elaborate Baroque decoration and a marble altar.
Continue in the same direction until you reach Chiesa di San Giuseppe.

2 Chiesa di San Giuseppe (Church of St Joseph)

The early 18th-century church hosted the chapels of many of Crotone's noble families. Its late Baroque sandstone façade features a wooden door framed by two pilasters with pretty capitals, and two tiled domes. Inside are three decorated stucco naves and some interesting wooden sculptures and 18th-century canvases.
Continue along this street for 100m (110yds) until just before the road turns, becoming Via Risorgimento. The Museo Archeologico Nazionale is directly in front and Villa Berlingieri is on the right.

3 Villa Berlingieri

Once the home of one of Crotone's most influential noble families, Villa Berlingieri ('Bastion of the Walls') was built in 1882. It has an elegant neoclassical façade and lovely garden.
Enter the Museo Archeologico Nazionale, directly in front.

4 Museo Archeologico Nazionale (National Archaeology Museum)

This excellent museum boasts an outstanding archaeological collection (*see p111 & p116*).
Continue along Via Risorgimento for 200m (220yds) to Piazza Castello. Palazzo Lucifero and Palazzo Morelli will be on your left and the castle on your right.

5 Castello Carlo V (Charles V Castle)

Cross the bridge to explore the ramparts and bastions of this majestic castle and enjoy the lovely views from the bridge back to the old town (*see p111*).
Cross Piazza Castello in the direction of the MACK at Palazzo Barracco.

6 Museo Arte Contemporanea (MACK, Museum of Contemporary Art) and Palazzo Barracco

The MACK (*see p116*) occupies elegant Palazzo Barracco, former residence of one of Italy's most fascinating noble families.
Facing Piazza Castello, take Vico Montalcino, then turn left. Here you'll find the dilapidated Palazzo Sculco, and,

further on, Casa Turano. Take the narrow steps to Via Pitagora.

7 Via Pitagora

This atmospheric alleyway allows you to peek inside people's homes, giving you an insight into their everyday life.
Follow Via Pitagora to Piazza Duomo.

8 Cattedrale (Cathedral), Piazza Duomo

Most of Crotone's imposing white cathedral was built in the 15th and 16th centuries, although parts of it also date from the 9th century. Austere on the outside, its interior is Baroque featuring beautiful marble and splendid paintings including *Our Lady of Capo Colonna*.

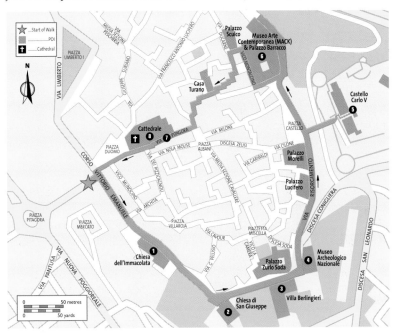

Aspects of archaeology

Calabria may not boast vast Pompeii-like ruins or splendid temples such as those at Agrigento in Sicily, but the region is home to important archaeological sites at Sibari, Locri and Capo Colonna – they just require a lot more imagination than most to appreciate them!

Locri Epizefiri is probably the most impressive and best-known site. Founded in the 8th century BC by colonists from Locri in central Greece, it's famous for the written laws developed there, considered to be the oldest of the Greek civilisation. While

Doric temple column, Hera Lacinia

it's one of the most studied sites, and despite its significance and vast size (95ha/235 acres), there's little for the untrained eye to appreciate. Indeed, unless you're an amateur archaeologist, you may want to leave Calabria's ruins off your itinerary altogether and concentrate instead on the superb, albeit compact, archaeological museums.

Home to outstanding collections of precious relics, such as the two striking 5th-century BC Bronzi di Riace (Riace bronzes) statues, Calabria's archaeological museums will give you a wonderful insight into the rich Magna Graecia ('Greater Greece') civilisation that flourished on the Italian peninsula for so many centuries. While there have been some archaeological digs in the Bova Marina area that have unearthed remnants of Neolithic and Bronze Age periods, they are nowhere near as impressive as the remarkable Magna Graecia discoveries.

The Magna Graecia period began in the 8th century BC after communities from cities on mainland Greece established colonies in Calabria, then known as Enotria or Italy. The waves of migration were motivated partly

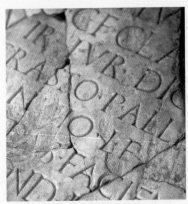

An artefact at the Museo Archeologico Nazionale Vito Capialbi

from a need to escape adversities such as overpopulation, overcrowding, social tensions and famine, and partly from the desire to develop trade and new opportunities for agricultural production. The site was chosen on the advice of the Oracle of Delphi.

The period would become one of the most prosperous for the Greeks and probably for Calabria historically, as there has never been an era that has produced such astonishing wealth, splendid art and culture, or so many sporting heroes. The first places settled were Rhegion (Reggio) in 743 BC, followed by Sybaris (Sibari) in 720 BC, Kroton (Crotone) in 710 BC and Lokroi Epizephyroi (Locri) between 710 BC and 690 BC. However, the whole of Calabria would eventually become Greek, with colonies developing at Krimisa (Cirò), Hipponion (Vibo Valentia), Metauros (Gioia Tauro) and Scolacium (Squillace).

After the decline of the Greek civilisation, the area would prosper once again under the Romans, who began arriving in 290 BC. But no period would ever be as rich and produce such beauty and splendour as the Magna Graecia civilisation.

The Museo Nazionale di Reggio Calabria is home to some of the most impressive pieces of the period. Aside from the magnificent Bronzi di Riace, there is the astounding 6th-century BC Testa di Filosofo (Head of the Philosopher) – notable for the extraordinary detail in the beard and hair as well as the emotion in the eyes – and beautiful coins and votive tablets.

Other outstanding museums include the Museo Archeologico Nazionale in Crotone, the Museo Nazionale Archeologico della Sibaritide at Sibari, and the Museo Archeologico Nazionale Vito Capialbi in the Norman castle at Vibo Valentia. The Museo Archeologico Nazionale in Crotone features treasures from Santuario di Hera Lacinia, including a magnificent gold crown with intertwined fig and myrtle leaves from the Temple of Hera along with pretty bronze statuettes of a sphinx and winged horse.

Age coins, bronzes, terracotta urns and vases, ceramics and other treasures, with its most impressive room showing precious finds from the Temple of Hera. *Via Risorgimento. Tel: (0962) 230 82. Open: Tue–Sun 9am–7.30pm. Admission charge.*

Museo Arte Contemporanea (MACK, Museum of Contemporary Art)

This new museum is home to an engaging exhibition of contemporary art, with work by some of the region's and Italy's most cutting-edge artists. *Palazzo Barracco, Piazza Castello 20. Tel: (0962) 905 714. Open: Mon–Fri 9.30am–1pm, Sat–Sun 10.30am–12.30pm. Free admission.*

Capo Rizzuto

Follow the seaside promenade southeast of Crotone and continue along the sandy beach, and after around 9km (5½ miles) you'll reach the plains that mark the beginning of the ancient promontory of Lacinium, now known as Capo Rizzuto (Cape Rizzuto). An otherwise dry landscape, the peninsula is blessed by a series of small bays with sandy beaches backed by pines, junipers, rock roses and aromatic thyme, and accessible only by narrow tracks and by boat. Parking here is next to impossible in summer.

Most of the area is now a protected marine and nature park, the **Area Marina Protetta Capo Rizzuto**, and is

Crotone's Castello Carlo V is an imposing structure

home to the Museo del Parco Archeologico di Capo Colonna, on the northeast tip of the promontory. There is an aquarium that is part of the park on a smaller peninsula at the promontory's southernmost tip also known as Capo Rizzuto, which juts dramatically into the cobalt-blue Ionian Sea and the Gulf of Squillace. West of this cape is Le Castella, an imposing Aragonese castle.

On land the Area Marina Protetta Capo Rizzuto doesn't appear terribly exciting, but offshore the sea is rich with diverse underwater flora and fauna, including vast fields of *Posidonia oceanica* seagrass, and is home to unique species of micro-organisms, loggerhead turtles, parrot fish, groupers, barracuda and dolphins as well as ancient archaeological treasures. As you arrive from Crotone, at the start of the cape you'll catch a glimpse of a beautiful rocky cove and beach below on your left before reaching Capo Colonna (Column Cape), the easternmost point of Calabria, and the Museo del Parco Archeologico di Capo Colonna.

Capo Colonna

While the image of the lone column of Capo Colonna standing dramatically in isolation on a windswept headland still graces Calabria's tourism brochures, these days the setting isn't nearly so romantic. Hidden beyond a sprawling car park, surrounded by overgrown grass and wire fencing, the single

surviving 8.3m (27ft) high column of the Doric temple of Hera Lacinia is now somewhat difficult to locate and appreciate.

Within the grounds of the Museo del Parco Archeologico di Capo Colonna, the column can be visited without buying a museum ticket, although the ticket gets you slightly closer. There's a stone watchtower (1550) nearby and next to it the red-roofed, whitewashed Chiesetta della Madonna di Capo Colonna, dating from 1519.

Le Castella/Castello Aragonese (Aragonese Castle)

Spectacularly situated on a tiny isle near the town of Isola di Capo Rizzuto, this splendid castle appears to float at sea. Visit either early morning or late afternoon to see it at its most stunning, when its sandstone bricks take on a golden glow. Framed with the turquoise-emerald sea and the cacti on the slopes in the foreground, it really is a magnificent sight.

'Le Castella' is actually several castles in one. All its former names are in the plural – Le Mura di Annibale ('Walls of Hannibal'), Torre della Castelli ('Tower of the Castles') and Castelli a Mare ('Castles in the Sea') – because what you see is actually an amalgamation of many castles. A substantial portion of the fortress was built at the end of the 13th century by the Angevins to defend themselves from attacks by the Arab raiders, including the high cylindrical tower, featuring a stone spiral staircase connecting three floors. The Angevins had incorporated walls dating from the Greek period of the 4th and 3rd centuries BC, although there are also remnants of Roman masonry. Most of what you see today, however, is Aragonese. The castle was given by Federico d'Aragona in 1496 to Andrea Carafa, who later restored it along with other castles in the area between 1510 and 1526.

Castle lovers will want to clamber about inside a bit, although there is little to see. Most visitors will be satisfied with a walk around the perimeter of the walls and the superb vistas of the castle from the shore. In front of Le Castella, at a depth

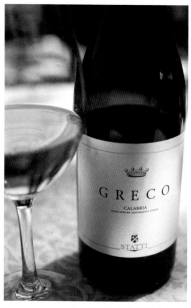

Greco grapes produce the best of Calabria's white wines

CALABRIAN WINE

Calabrian wines are hard to find on Italian tables outside Calabria, let alone on wine lists around the world, but they're one of the region's best-kept secrets. The reason is that most of the grapes are sent off to prop up and give body to wines made further north. Most grapes are of the Gaglioppo variety, used to make red wines, while the dominant white wine grape is Greco di Bianco, used to produce a sweet white. Both varieties are of Greek origin. Cirò is the most visible of the wine-growing regions, and its heavy reds are a local speciality.

of 24m (79ft), there is the wreck of the ship *Gunny*, which sank here in 1962.

Isola di Capo Rizzuto. Tel: (0962) 795 511. Open: Jul–Sept daily 9am–1pm (last entrance 12.30pm); Oct–Jun Tue–Sun 9am–1pm & 2–6pm. Admission charge (includes guide).

Museo del Parco Archeologico di Capo Colonna (Capo Colonna Archaeological Park Museum)

The small museum in a sleek contemporary building is situated within the 40ha (99-acre) archaeological park and nature reserve. Once an important sanctuary dedicated to Hera Lacinia, the goddess of fertility and pastures, it boasted a magnificent temple set within thick wooded forests. Sadly, all that is left now is a single column (*see p118*).

The museum features three themed exhibitions displaying treasures from ancient Kroton: 'The Earth', 'The

Sacred' and 'The Sea'. 'The Earth' traces the history of the sanctuary from its establishment in 194 BC to its demise in the 1st century AD, and includes the terracotta bust of an unidentified Roman divinity, ceramics used in the homes of noblemen, and displays of splendid coins. 'The Sacred' focuses on the sanctuary itself and features beautiful marble and terracotta sculptures, votive stones and portions of the temple ceiling and structure.

'The Sea' features relics that have been found underwater off the coast here in recent years. Calabria's Ionian coastline was a bridge between the eastern and western Mediterranean, Sicily and Africa, and was used by ancient ships transporting agricultural products as well as raw and manufactured materials. As a result, shapeless pieces of marble, massive marble columns, bases for statues, lion's paws and votive stones have all been found on the seabed.

Viale Magna Grecia, Capo Colonna. Tel: (0962) 934 814. www.fondazioneodyssea.it. Open: Jul–Sept Tue–Sun 9am–1.30pm & 3.30–8pm; Oct–Jun Tue–Sun 9am–1pm & 3–7pm. Admission charge for museum.

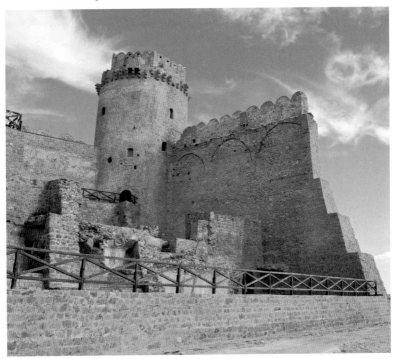

The ruins of Le Castella

Getting away from it all

Good motorways (autostrade) *and trunk roads may well criss-cross Calabria, yet just a short distance from those busy thoroughfares, as the crow flies, are somnolent villages that seem to be lost in time, tranquil lakeside retreats that appear to be abandoned, walking trails through dense forests, and overgrown roads that apparently lead nowhere, all making ideal destinations for getting away from it all.*

Exploring Calabria's national parks

Calabria's three main national parks – Pollino in the north, La Sila in the centre and the Aspromonte in the south – are all wonderful to explore, whether it's from behind the wheels of a car, by foot on an organised hike, on the back of a horse, or on a mountain-biking excursion. These glorious natural playgrounds offer everything from trekking and canyoning to fishing and canoeing or skiing and snowboarding.

One of the most pleasurable ways to experience Calabria's national parks, however, is traipsing through the canopied forests, across earth covered with fragrant pine needles and speckled with light, or rambling over the rolling hills with their gentle grassy slopes.

In the Sila there are compelling walks through the idyllic countryside where you'll find ancient sky scraping trees with colossal girths to hug, and serene lakes where you can row a boat or cast

a rod. In the Aspromonte you can exert a bit more energy on a one-day hike or seven-day trek that will take you to cascading waterfalls shaded by prehistoric ferns, or enjoy splendid views all the way to Etna in Sicily. In Pollino, Italy's largest national park, you can admire the rare Bosnian pine, in one of the last places it grows in Italy, and with binoculars do your best to spot the park's wonderful wildlife, including the Italian wolf, the European otter, wild boar and birds such as the black woodpecker, peregrine falcon and Egyptian vulture.

Without going to too much trouble, you can enjoy countryside blanketed with the vibrant wild flowers that are characteristic of the Mediterranean, especially in spring but also in summer, from the bright yellow broom flowers to the colourful pink, white and yellow clusters of the mimosa shrub. You'll also get to drink in the scent of citrus, rosemary, thyme and almond, the delicious taste of the fruit from the mulberry and fig trees, and the arresting images of the strange red aloe plant and the agave cacti growing wild, a typical sight in the mountains of the Ionian coast and particularly stunning when in full bloom. If you're lucky, you may even stumble across some *fungi porcini*, but don't pick mushrooms unless you're sure you know what they are.

All through the national parks there are walking trails that begin on the main driving routes through the parks, where you can pull over, get your bearings from the 'maps' carved out on wooden boards posted at the start of the trail, and head off for a short stroll or a longer hike. Ensure you take the necessary precautions: let your hotel know what you are doing, be

adequately equipped, and carry plenty of water and snacks.

If you read Italian, for the Sila National Park you can pick up a copy of the booklet *A Piedi in Sila Grande* (*On Foot in Sila Grande*) from the Pro Loco tourist office in Camigliatello (*see p169*) or from one of the national park offices; there is one at Lago Cecita and one at Taverna. The book outlines 12 different itineraries, although there are apparently over 30 you can do.

For Aspromonte National Park you can buy a copy of *Il Parco Nazionale d'Aspromonte: Guida Naturalistica ed Escursionistica* from most museum bookshops, which outlines 53 itineraries, ranging from easy one-hour walks to more strenuous seven-hour hikes. Both books grade the routes by

Horses run free in Sila National Park

Wild flowers cover the hillsides during spring in the Aspromonte National Park

difficulty, include altitude details, durations and map references, advise on the best time of year to go, provide road directions for getting to the start of the routes, and then describe the routes in some detail. Alternatively, you can hire a guide or join an excursion, for which the Pro Loco offices have details.

Drives off the beaten track

Travellers intent on getting away from it all in Calabria should begin by hiring a car for some off-the-beaten-track drives. Aside from the weekend, when the whole of Calabria seems to take to the road, you'll see few other people once you get off the main roads, and there are some routes where you won't see another soul for hours.

In the Aspromonte, one of the least-travelled routes begins at the turn-off from the town of Melito di Porto Salvo, on the coast 30km (19 miles) south of Reggio, and passes through the villages of Chorio, Bagaladi and Croce di Romeo, taking you along an extremely narrow and very winding road with lots of hairpin turns. While you'll occasionally pass a farmer on a tractor or a shepherd guiding his sheep, the route appears to be little used, with weeds growing through cracks in the bitumen and the bends in the road overgrown with long grass. The scenery is spectacular (*see pp48–9*).

Another little-travelled road runs along the perimeter of the Pollino from Belvedere Marittimo, via San'Agata di Esaro, San Sosti and Acquaformosa to

Lungro. Here the highlight is the impenetrable vegetation, almost rainforest-like in parts, and the multitude of wild flowers. Wind down your window and breathe in the fragrant aromas.

The Sila offers up a number of driving routes that pass beneath canopies of overhanging trees, skirt the shores of serene lakes and cruise through scenic pastoral settings, but one of the least-travelled roads is just outside the national park. From San Giovanni in Fiore, a narrow, twisting road meanders along the mountainside via Savelli, Verzino and Umbriatico to Cirò, passing through splendid, wild country and ramshackle old villages that see few foreigners from one year to the next. Here, people *will* stop and stare at you, but return their hostile glares with a wave and you might be pleasantly surprised to receive a smile in return.

For any mountainous drives, it's important to rent an economy-sized car with some grunt: you'll encounter lots of winding roads with steep gradients and sharp corners to negotiate, and many of the routes become one-way roads high in the mountains (especially in the Aspromonte), so, if ever you have to pull over, you'll need a small car to ensure you're completely off the road.

Note that all too often a main road that takes you through a village will quickly become a narrow one-way alley barely wide enough for one car, let alone two. Once you're in the historical centre of a medieval village, there will

Getting away from it all

On the road in Sila National Park

A shepherd moves his flock in the Aspromonte

generally be a few tight squeezes and it will be next to impossible to turn around if you get in a jam.

Remote villages

Calabria's 'remote' villages might not be far-flung and they are not isolated as far as distances are concerned, but they are worlds away in terms of their everyday culture and lifestyle when compared to the region's cities and seaside resorts. Many older locals would argue that it's only in the villages that you'll find the authentic Calabria.

In southern Calabria, in lightly populated stone villages such as Roghudi in the Aspromonte, time moves at a snail's pace, while in nearby hamlets such as Casalnuovo, a virtual ghost town, tiny Staiti and diminutive Condofuri, time seems to stand completely still. You can drive to these quaint villages along extremely narrow, meandering roads, and, while it's much more fun to trek between them, there are very few facilities in the villages themselves and they are not used to welcoming strangers.

Further north, on the back roads between Amantea and Cosenza, you'll find a similar sense of isolation and a certain charm in the alluring villages of Terrati, Lago and Potame, all of which perch dramatically on mountainsides overlooking spectacular scenery, yet you won't experience the same kind of hostility. Here, old village women wear headscarves and long skirts and comb the hills in search of wild herbs while their elderly husbands carry firewood down the road on the backs of donkeys.

Very few of these villages are equipped for tourists. It's rare they'll have a local shop to provide basic necessities, let alone a restaurant where you might buy lunch or a service station to refuel, so ensure you have a full tank of petrol and plan your day accordingly. While the villages might not seem far away as the crow flies, the distances can be deceptive, especially if you're climbing to high altitudes, and the going will be slow on many of the more meandering roads.

If these communities are a little too rustic and remote for you, yet you still want to get a feel for Calabrian village life, visit the slightly larger villages and small towns that are closer to cities and therefore more developed. The captivating medieval village of Santa Severina, not far from Crotone, boasts a lovely piazza and splendid cathedral and castle, while it is also worth exploring the Albanian villages of the Cosenza region such as San Demetrio Corone, home to impressive Norman-Byzantine architecture and offering stunning vistas of the surrounding lush countryside.

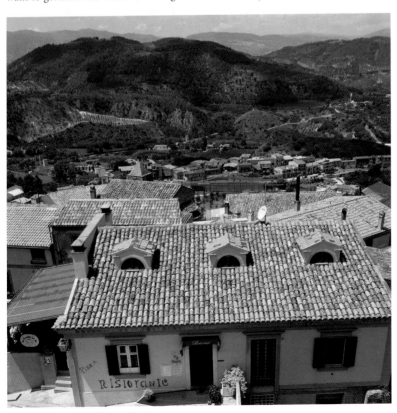

Views from the castle of Santa Severina

When to go

Calabria is a year-round destination, which means there's plenty to see and do whenever you go there. Spring and autumn are ideal times to visit, when the weather is comfortably warm and there's a beautiful clarity to the light. Italian sun-worshippers prefer the scorching summer, while winter-sports fans flock to the mountains during the often too-short winter. Whichever season you choose, make sure you bring the right clothes: it can be freezing in the mountains in winter and blazingly hot on the beaches in summer.

Spring

When the snow starts to melt and the wild flowers make their appearance, the mountains beckon. Spring is a great time for a hiking holiday, especially late spring after the snow pack has reduced. Serra San Bruno and the Pollino, Aspromonte and Sila national parks are all wonderful spots to head to. The air is crisp in the mornings, and the evenings can be chilly, yet the days can be positively balmy, more akin to northern European summers. In early spring the waterfront restaurants awake from winter hibernation, while late in spring the beach resorts begin to open their shutters and slap on fresh coats of paint, and at the lidos they start wiping down the deckchairs. The summer crowds have not yet arrived, so room rates can be bargained down, and, while the water is brisk, at least the beaches haven't yet become an endless sea of bodies.

Summer

Destinations such as Tropea, Pizzo and Scilla and the various lidos on the east coast are magic during summer.
But be warned: it's scorching, and uncomfortably so away from the beach. If you're lucky to get a booking,

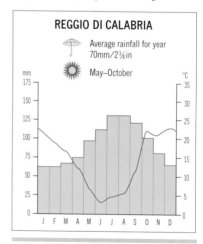

REGGIO DI CALABRIA

Average rainfall for year
70mm/2¾in

May–October

WEATHER CONVERSION CHART

25.4mm = 1 inch
°F = 1.8 × °C + 32

A burst of spring colour in Sila National Park

however, a long summer evening spent watching the sunset with a bottle of white and seafood aplenty is hard to beat after a hard day swimming and sunbathing on the sandy beaches. For Tropea, you must book months in advance for summer. Many Italians have standing annual bookings. Avoid August, when the whole of Italy is on holiday and the beaches, bars and restaurants are overflowing.

Autumn

After the summer hordes have departed, the secret in Calabria is that the water temperature is still agreeable and, because the locals' thoughts have turned to the upcoming football season, the beaches are blissfully empty and restaurants easier to drop into without a booking – especially during the week. Early autumn is ideal, when the weather has cooled down enough to make camping and hiking a pleasant experience. By late autumn, the leaves are changing colour, and driving, horse riding and picnicking in the mountains are a delight.

Winter

Winter in Calabria is one of the least popular seasons for foreign tourists, but locals know that the mountains are especially wonderful then. There are plenty of cross-country and downhill skiing opportunities and lots of excuses to sit by a fire and sip red wine while snacking on local cheeses, spicy sausages and hearty pastas! December and January have the most rain, but at least this translates to snow in the mountains.

Getting around

If you're intending to take a sightseeing trip around Calabria, it's best (and most easily) done by car, but if you're on a tight budget and have specific destinations that you want to visit, Italy's vast train system can work to your advantage. Both forms of transport offer scenic vistas, but travelling by car is considerably more straightforward, especially if you take into account the convenience of the autostrada.

Driving

Car hire

It's always best to book rental cars in advance for Calabria, as cars in all categories are often thin on the ground. Also, booking your hire car when you book your flight is often a good way to get a discounted daily rate. EU-licensed drivers need only their own current driving licence. Drivers from other countries need to check with the rental agency as to whether they need an International Driving Permit, usually available through your national automobile association.

Driving conditions

There are four main ways to drive to Calabria. The A3 *autostrada* from Naples runs right down to Reggio di Calabria and is an excellent road. A coast road roughly hugs the west coast down to Reggio, as does a similar road down the less visited east coast. Minor roads also zigzag their way through the mountainous national parks and, while picturesque, should be tackled in small doses – in no small part because of the locals' habit of choosing the straightest line through the bends rather than sticking to their own side of the road. Ensure that your hire car has a working horn!

Generally, the more minor the road the slower you'll go, and the more minor the road the less maintenance it will have received. If you are heading into the mountains, choose a vehicle with a decent amount of horsepower, but keep in mind that a narrow economy-sized car is far better for navigating village streets that were literally made for a donkey and cart to pass through.

Rules of the road

In Italy you drive on the right side of the road. When on an *autostrada*, keep to the right to allow faster vehicles to overtake on the left. Unless you are on a roundabout (where those already on it have the right of way), vehicles on your right have right of way. Speed limits are 130kph (81mph) on the *autostrade*, 110kph (68mph) on main roads, 90kph (56mph) on rural roads and 50kph (31mph) through residential areas. The blood-alcohol content limit is 0.5g.

Train travel

Trains are a common way to travel in Italy and, apart from the occasional strike, don't do a bad job of getting people around the country. While many travellers frequently take the train from Naples to Palermo (in Sicily), the intercity trains stop at some of Calabria's best spots, such as Amantea, Pizzo, Reggio di Calabria, Scilla and Tropea. Reservations are a sound idea, as the trains get crowded, especially in summer. Trains are also a fine way to arrive in Calabria from other parts of the country. For instance, an intercity train from Rome to Tropea takes around six hours. Always confirm that the trains are running before heading to the station – just in case. For more information, visit TrenItalia's website: *www.ferroviedellostato.it*

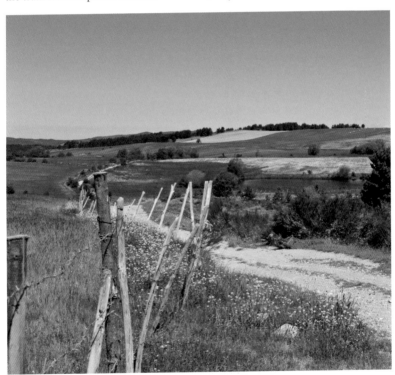

Some country roads may be little more than tracks

Accommodation

Calabria is Italy's least-visited tourist region, so don't expect to see five-star hotel brands at every stop. There simply aren't any big-name hotels, and in fact there are very few five-star hotels of the quality you find elsewhere in Italy. What Calabria excels in are small, charming hotels in historic buildings, including plenty of former palazzi, baronial lodges and bed and breakfasts (B&Bs) offering oodles of atmosphere, abundant personal service and a memorable once-in-a-lifetime experience.

Calabria boasts summer beach resorts, hilltop towns, mountain villages and five provincial capitals, all of which are home to mainly three- and four-star properties. In summer hotspots such as Tropea, and to a lesser extent Pizzo, you'll find a reasonable range of accommodation, while in small towns such as Gerace, Altomonte and Morano Calabro there will be only a couple of options. In the region's biggest city, Reggio di Calabria, you'll find everything from five stars to excellent B&Bs, but here you need to book ahead as the city hosts plenty of conferences and events, when everything in town fills up.

In terms of quality of service, Calabria tends not to be as advanced as other more visited areas in Italy, such as Tuscany. Given that there are no big chain hotels operating here, the service you'll receive is purely reliant on the individual provider's attitude: you might be treated as family, but, conversely, you could be considered as just an interruption to a football match on TV.

Facilities and equipment standards in hotels tend to be lower than you'll find elsewhere in Italy. In Calabria you'll generally find rooms with tiny old televisions, empty rusted minibar fridges, and little in the way of other amenities. However, there are notable exceptions that have large flat-screen televisions, cable TV, Wi-Fi Internet and a decent bottle of *prosecco* (sparkling wine) in the fridge.

One thing to keep in mind if you're driving around Calabria is whether a hotel has parking, and, if it does, whether it's secure or on the street, and whether there is an extra charge for this. Some towns don't allow parking near the centre for non-resident vehicles, and often hotels are not interested in lugging your bags – you'll generally do this yourself. Always check these details when booking the hotel, and, while you might not have any other accommodation choices in that town, you can at least be prepared and the experience of parking will be less stressful.

Booking ahead is always a good idea, especially if you are travelling to the beach in summer or the mountains in winter. Local annual returnees can book up summer hotspots such as Pizzo, Scilla and Tropea in summer, especially in August, and turning up in these places during the hotter months without a booking is not advised.

Many places do have websites through which you can make a booking, but you'll find that sometimes the level of English, both written and spoken, can be a problem. It's best always to confirm your booking by phone as well and have printouts of any confirmations handy when you check in.

Accommodation

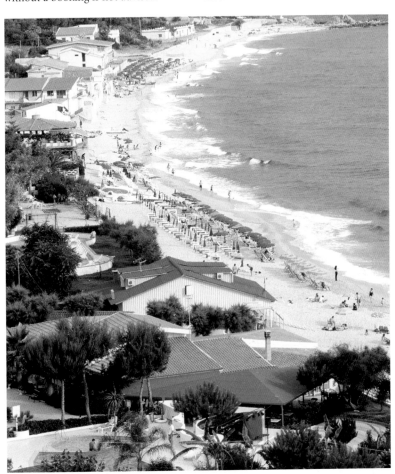

Umbrellas line the beach at Capo Vaticano

Food and drink

The cuisine of the south of Italy is a delight. While there are many dishes that are ubiquitous across Italy, such as the use of pasta and obligatory pizza, nearly every Italian dish can be traced to a particular region. Central to the cuisine of the south is the notion of cucina povera *(peasant cooking), where you make do with what you have, from making pasta from chestnut flour to utilising every bit of an animal that is slaughtered (which explains dishes such as tripe).*

Calabrian cuisine

The apparent simplicity of the cuisine disguises the inventiveness that the Calabrians have applied to their cooking, as well as just how healthy the Mediterranean diet is, with its fantastic olive oil and fresh vegetables and fruits as key components. But, at its soul, Calabrian cuisine is, above all, rustic, hearty and honest.

Foreign invaders have had a huge impact on Calabrian, and also Sicilian, cooking. The Arabs brought spices, fruits and, some argue, pasta to the region. Traces of French, Jewish and Spanish influences are also evident.

Given Calabria's access to the sea, both *spada* (swordfish) and *tonno* (tuna) feature heavily, sometimes eaten as *carpaccio* (raw), in pastas or as 'steaks' for main courses. The most popular vegetable is *melanzana* (aubergine or eggplant), which is marinated, grilled or stuffed – any way you have it will be a delight. This is matched in popularity only by the onions of the Tropea region, which are sweet and tasty. Lamb is popular. Cow's cheeses, such as the delicious *caciocavallo*, are excellent fresh but also fabulous grilled. Figs and nuts feature heavily as well, as do all types of melons.

But one thing that sets Calabrian cuisine apart from that of other Italian regions is the use of *peperoncino* (chilli pepper). Local chillies come in various shapes and sizes but are generally spicy hot. They are used fresh, dried or preserved in olive oil, flavour everything from cured meats to pasta sauces, and make a brilliant chilli oil.

Vegetarian options

Vegetarians eat well in Italy, with menus featuring plenty of pizzas and pastas that don't contain *carne* (meat) and are just as tasty as those that do. Grilled vegetables and salads, as well as bean dishes, are readily available and are delicious. Vegans, however, will find it harder going.

Eateries

Typically, a *ristorante* is the most elegant and expensive of Italy's eateries, and a trattoria is a more casual version of a *ristorante*. Both are generally open for lunch and dinner. An *osteria* is a small eatery with a short, locally focused menu and a good wine list, quite often open only for dinner, while an *enoteca* is a wine bar that also serves snacks and perhaps two or three meals and is usually open at the owner's whim, but always in the evening. These days in Italy the hierarchy of eateries is not an indication of quality. An *enoteca* can often be the best place to eat in town, and an *osteria* may offer the most adventurous menu. In Calabria the dress code is generally smart casual, but for Italian men this will often mean a jacket, even if it's matched with jeans and a T-shirt. At beachside locations, lunch is casual, but there'll be an expectation that you'll return to your hotel to shower and change for dinner. Always reserve a table if there are more than six in a party.

Food and drink

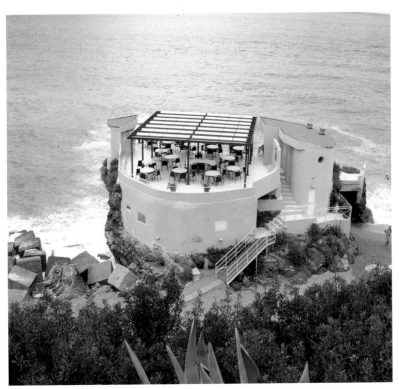

A unique restaurant takes advantage of the views in Cosenza

Food and drink

Meal times

Breakfast (*la colazione*) is generally served from 7am until 10.30am, but if you're looking for a café dead on 7am you'll be lucky to find a warm coffee machine in town. As Italians eat a light breakfast – usually a pastry and coffee – you won't find much more than this on

Calabria's best: red wine from Cirò

offer at all but top-end hotels. Lunch (*il pranzo*) generally runs from noon until 2pm, although at seaside towns they may take orders until 3pm. For many locals this is *the* big meal of the day (it certainly is at weekends), consisting of at least two or three courses, so don't be annoyed if a waiter acts surprised when you order just one dish. Dinner (*la cena*) is usually served from 7pm until 10–10.30pm, and, unless it's a celebration, for Italians this usually consists of just a couple of courses. Locals tend to eat late, arriving as the tourists are finishing! Outside lunch and dinner, panini (basically toasted sandwiches) are available from cafés and some bars. Stand-alone pizzerie (the takeaway variety) are often open for lunch or from around 4pm until late.

Menus

When eating in a *ristorante* or a trattoria and sometimes an *osteria*, you'll find the menu split up into several courses. You might be offered an *aperitivo* such as Campari to start with or some *prosecco* (sparkling wine). The first course on the menu is antipasto (literally meaning 'before the meal'), typically consisting of cured meats and cheeses or bruschetta (toasted bread with olive oil and toppings). Primo is the first course, consisting of pasta, risotto or a hearty soup. Secondo (second course) is the main dish, usually meat or fish reared or caught locally. As the meat or fish dish is often served without any starch or extra

vegetables, a *contorno* (side dish of cooked vegetables) features on the menu. A *formaggio* (cheese) course may be offered next, before dolce (dessert), *caffè* (coffee) and a *digestivo* (shot of liqueur such as grappa or limoncello), which, if you've managed to get through all those courses, will probably be on the house!

While it's normal to have one quick course at an *enoteca* or an *osteria*, most people will have a couple of courses at a *ristorante* or a trattoria, generally antipasto and pasta, a pasta and main, or a main and dolce for those with a sweet tooth. If you're making a booking at a *ristorante* or a trattoria on a busy evening, it's expected that you'll have at least two or three courses.

Restaurant tipping

You will often find a *coperto* (cover charge) of one or two euros on *il conto* (the bill). This is for water and bread and is not a tip. If *servizio* is included, no tipping is necessary, but otherwise tip up to 10 per cent for good service.

Shopping and markets

Compared to the rest of Italy, fresh food markets are modest in Calabria, and you'll find locals picking up fresh produce at a roadside stall or their local fruit and vegetable shop. There are superb delicatessens and wine shops in more popular destinations, such as Tropea, that have wonderful local wines and other produce.

Entertainment

Entertainment in Calabria is very much based around outdoor activities. Calabrians live by the edict that everything tastes better when taken alfresco. Long lunches into the late afternoon, dinners that see the hours and courses pass by, aperitivi *(pre-dinner drinks) on a terrace with friends, and gelato savoured while strolling along a seaside promenade – all these take up much of the leisure time in the south.*

In the larger provincial capitals of Reggio di Calabria, Cosenza, Catanzaro, Crotone and, to a lesser extent, Vibo Valentia, there are some live venues where theatre, jazz, rock, classical music and dance performances take place. However, when it comes to entertainment in Calabria, it's nature that takes centre stage – the beaches and mountains are the region's playground – so don't expect a calendar in any way comparable to those found in the north of Italy, where there are non-stop entertainment and cultural activities throughout the year. It's really only in summer that you'll find regular music festivals and concerts scheduled.

One of the most popular forms of entertainment in Calabria is the *passeggiata*, the outdoor evening stroll. Here it seems everyone has come out for their leisurely saunter up and down the main pedestrian shopping street or along the seaside promenade. In Calabria it's taken extremely seriously, and like clockwork an empty street is

suddenly crowded at around 5 or 6pm, a little later in summer. Everyone heads out, whole families, groups of teenagers, elderly couples linked arm in arm, and they're all out to see and be seen, stopping to chat with friends they might meet. For the young ones it's about flirting and showing off, for the older Calabrians it's an important part of their social life and for many it's the main form of entertainment.

Eating out

Cafés also form the backbone of Calabrian social life. The café that locals frequent is easy to identify: it's usually open long hours, has great coffee and a stand-up bar, and is a meeting point for friends who can sit for hours over an espresso, a small glass of water and perhaps a shot of local liqueur. This is where you'll find older men mid-morning enjoying a glass of wine or a summer beer. Older women often head to their favourite *gelateria*, where their partaking of the Italian ice

Calabrians enjoying their *passeggiata*

cream is a very serious affair: ordering can be a lengthy and animated process and is part of the entertainment factor of this local tradition.

In restaurants a long, leisurely meal is the norm for Calabrians, and here ordering and discussing the menu is most certainly part of the entertainment. Many questions are asked of the waiter, the owner, the chef or all three, about the freshness of the produce, where it came from, aspects of the cooking, the style of pasta and the ingredients in the sauces. *All*

Italians take their food seriously, and a debate over what pasta shape is best matched with a particular sauce can be a lively and lengthy discussion. For locals the restaurant experience is often the night's entertainment, except maybe for sampling a gelato on the way home, but you'll rarely see local Calabrians not take coffee, grappa or limoncello at the end of the meal.

Bars and clubs

Bars are often a male domain in Calabria and they tend to be the

Il Teatro Comunale Francesco Cilea hosts great jazz and other music in Reggio di Calabria

meeting place for local men in the late afternoon to discuss politics and football, although older, retired men can often be found frequenting them on a morning or two. They never linger long and they never drink too much; rather it's the social aspect of the visit that's important. For visitors many bars will not be particularly welcoming: the local men see their local bar as their own private boys' club. Women will feel more comfortable in an *enoteca* or *osteria*, where the wine is taken as seriously as the conversation, and these are far more relaxed places for visitors. However, unlike in the rest of Italy, you will only really find these wine bars in the more sophisticated cities of the region, such as Reggio di Calabria.

During summer, temporary bars and clubs make their appearance on the waterfront beside lidos, and in Calabria in late spring it's entertaining to watch how quickly some of these places are established. While some are nothing more than a flimsy open wooden bar with a plastic skirt and roof and a fridge-freezer, others are a lot more sophisticated. Calabrians can go to quite some length building a solid wooden structure, laying down flooring and roofing, slapping on several coats of paint and fitting it all out with chic furniture, filmy curtains and sexy lighting, only to pull it down at the end of the season. At the simpler versions of these beach bars you can get 'takeaway' beers and mixed

drinks in plastic cups, while at the more sophisticated ones you'll find a long list of cocktails. In terms of English-style pubs, you're pretty much out of luck outside Reggio di Calabria.

During summer, dance parties and DJ-driven events also make their appearance, generally held in temporary beachside clubs. These are especially popular in and around Reggio di Calabria, and at the lido-focused resorts on the coast.

Cinema and theatre

If you're looking to catch up on Italy's great history in film-making, you'll be sorely disappointed in Calabria. The local video stores are popular in this region for a reason: there are barely any cinemas outside Reggio di Calabria. If it's theatre or live performances of opera or ballet you're after, you'll find that, apart from one-off outdoor events, these are generally held only in the beautiful old theatres in Reggio di Calabria (Teatro Comunale Francesco Cilea) and Catanzaro (Teatro Politeama).

These venues also offer live jazz, which is of a very high standard in Italy. You'll also find live jazz in summer at the popular holiday destinations. Summer also sees plenty of cover bands playing Italian and international hits. Live, public, traditional music performances are, unfortunately, generally relegated to local celebrations and festivals.

Shopping

The Grand Tourists may have passed through Calabria on their way to Sicily, but modern tourism in the region is still fairly underdeveloped, so outside Tropea and Pizzo there is little in the way of souvenir shops or outlets selling handicrafts or other locally made products. What you will find if you look hard are some beautiful traditional textiles, splendid ceramics and rustic pottery. More widely available are edible souvenirs, including spicy 'nduja (Calabrian sausage), sweet liqueurs and liquorice.

Calabria has a long tradition of producing beautiful textiles. Catanzaro was once the silk capital of the world and it's still possible to find handmade linen and cotton. It's rare to stumble across an old lady at a loom as you might in Cyprus or Crete, but if you do you'd be wise to buy something. You will see some lovely rustic linen, cotton and wool bedcovers, sheets and cloth in neutral shades, many made in a rough-hewn style with sparse stripes. These are mostly made by **Fabbrica Tessile Bossio** (*Via P Mancini 3, Calopezzati, Cosenza. Tel: (0983) 442 46*) using traditional designs and techniques.

Other regional crafts you might see are hand-carved wood (especially salad servers and bowls) and wicker and straw products, including traditional brooms, brushes and baskets, which are being made again in villages such as Soriano Calabro.

Tropea and Pizzo certainly make up for what the other destinations lack, however, with whole streets dedicated to souvenirs. In Pizzo, Via San Francesco is the street to browse, while in Tropea you can look in the shops on Corso Vittorio Emanuele and Via R Margherita di Savoia, where you will find some beautiful things among the usual tourist tat.

Ceramics

Not all of what you'll find in Tropea and Pizzo is made in Calabria, but if you're not going anywhere else in Italy these are excellent places to pick up souvenirs such as the vibrant Moorish-influenced ceramics in bright blues and yellows, typically found in the south, that originally came from Sicily. Look out for beautiful bowls, plates, platters, vases, candlesticks and wine jugs. If you're worried about excess luggage, pretty ceramic tiles and candlesticks make great souvenirs that won't take up much space. The shop with the best selection is **La Vecchia Forgia Artigianato** (*Via Umberto I 4. Tel: (0963) 666 474*) in Tropea.

You will find some original handmade local pottery and ceramics as well, and one shop in Tropea that is exceptional is **Artigianato & Design by Macri** (*Via R Margherita di Savoia 34/36. Tel: 339 364 4446*), which sells strikingly beautiful pieces including enormous platters and urns with bold designs. Another shop, **L'Anfora** (*Piazza Ercole. Tel: (0963) 624 06*), stocks rustic farmhouse-style ceramics hand-painted with pretty designs featuring lemons, vegetables and flowers.

Chilli peppers

The *peperoncino* or chilli is a typical product of which all Calabrians are

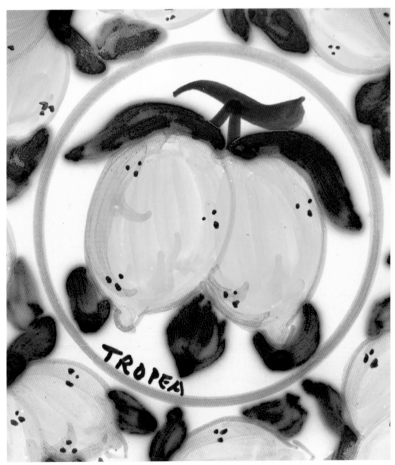

Ceramics like this from Tropea are a popular souvenir of the region

proud, and you'll see all sorts of arts and crafts bearing the red chilli pepper, from vibrantly painted ceramic plates and chilli-shaped ceramic salt and pepper pots to extravagant Murano-like glass chandeliers dripping with decorative bunches of tiny red peppers. One souvenir you'll see all over the region is a ceramic figurine of a Calabrian woman in a long traditional skirt covered in red peppers, holding a red pepper-shaped plate upon her head as she might hold a basket. It makes a pleasing memento.

Food and drink

The best Calabrian souvenirs are without a doubt the edible ones, and all

Grappa, flavoured with local bergamot

over the region you'll find fantastic shops specialising in *Prodotti Tipici Calabresi* (typical Calabrian products) including preserves (sun-dried tomatoes, courgettes, aubergines and peppers), *peperoncini* (dried, preserved in olive oil, and in paste and sauce form), *'nduja* (Calabria's unique, spicy chilli sausage paste), red Tropea onions (hanging in pretty bunches, or as a jarred relish or mousse), *fungi porcini* (porcini mushrooms), *miele* (honey), biscotti (typical crunchy Italian biscuits) and, of course, dried pasta.

You'll also see *radice di liquirizia* (raw liquorice), which is liquorice in its natural form (it looks like a bunch of small dried twigs), as well as Amarelli's famous flavoured pastels in retro tins, liquorice syrup-centred chocolates and liquorice liqueurs. While many shops throughout the region sell Amarelli's delicious products, the gift shop at the factory and museum in Rossano has by far the widest range.

In addition to liquorice liqueurs, other alcoholic souvenirs include Greco di Bianco, a famous liqueur made from the Greco grape from Bianco near Reggio di Calabria, Passito Moscato, a very sweet dessert wine, and limoncello, which is more typically associated with the island of Capri and the Amalfi coast.

Bergamoto or bergamot, a citrus fruit peculiar to Calabria, is another speciality that comes in many different shapes and forms, including bergamot-flavoured cakes and biscuits (*berghiotti*), bergamot liqueur and, of course, bergamot perfume. Look for the bergamot cologne in retro packaging, a classic, old-fashioned fragrance in the style of those our grandmothers used to dab on their wrists.

Again, the narrow cobblestone streets of Tropea and Pizzo are crammed with shops overflowing with these delectable goodies. The best in Tropea, if not the region, is **Pane e Sale**, meaning 'Bread and Salt' (*Via Stazione 1. Tel: (0963) 666 350*). Here, the knowledgeable English-speaking staff will offer you tasty morsels of some of the more mouthwatering and most interesting treats you'll find in Calabria, including biscotti flavoured with pepper and chocolate, and fragrant honey scented with pepper, acacia or *fiori della Calabria* (Calabrian flowers).

In Pizzo the shelves of **Museo del Peperoncino** (*Via San Francesco 6. Tel: 333 579 1845*) are crammed with similar typical products, as is the tiny shop in Reggio di Calabria called **Pizzimenti** (*Via Fata Morgana 46. Tel: (0965) 331 604*) and **Sapori e Gusti Mediterranei** in Morano Calabro (*Via Martiri della Libertà 2/1. Tel: (0981) 399 812*). In Camigliatello the long main street is lined with shops selling preserves, wines, cheeses and cold cuts, the last being vacuum-packed to enable safe transportation home. Rossano, Gerace, Cosenza and Crotone all have similar shops.

Sport and leisure

Yes, there is more to Calabria than just lazing around on the beach. There are numerous watersports, as well as hiking, biking and skiing scenes, which take full advantage of Calabria's crystal-clear waters, clean air and pristine mountains. Italians love outdoor sports, and Italy is, overall, a very fit nation compared to other Western countries. Italians stay fit in myriad ways, and for Calabrians it's cycling and walking that are the most popular means of maintaining la bella figura *('the beautiful figure').*

Cycling

Calabria is excellent for bike touring, and, despite their reputation for erratic driving, Calabrians are well used to bikers on the road. The options are endless, although the mountains can be quite daunting, and not really made for those packing a month's worth of gear. Both the east and west coasts make for fascinating touring, the west coast boasting more scenic diversions, especially around Tropea and Capo Vaticano. If it's the rush of mountain biking you're after, Camigliatello (the most popular ski resort) has paths that will get your adrenalin going.

Diving

You might not rise to the surface with the missing Riace bronze (*see p28*), but you will see plenty underwater in Calabria, including lots of ancient wrecks. Calabria has some of the best diving conditions on the Italian Mediterranean, especially in the provinces of Vibo Valentia and Reggio di Calabria. Water temperatures are pleasant and visibility is very good. Tropea and Capo Vaticano are two popular diving centres, and many diving companies offer PADI (Professional Association of Diving Instructors) diving courses as well as offshore trips for experienced divers. Reefs, masses of vegetation and plenty of sea life are on offer, with visibility of up to 30m (98ft) not uncommon owing to the constant currents and lack of polluting big industry in the area.

Football

This being Italy, football (soccer to some nations) is always the hottest topic of conversation and the greatest sporting interest. Of the 20 clubs in Serie A (Italy's premier league), only one is from Calabria, Reggina Calcio. Nicknamed *amaranto* (dark-reds, their home colour), they have lived up to Calabria's corrupt reputation by being indicted in the 2006 Serie A match-fixing scandal. Despite this, they've managed to hold on to their place in Serie A, but rarely trouble the leading clubs. They play at the 28,000-seat Stadio Oreste Granillo. Their traditional rivals, Sicily's Messina, just a short ferry ride away, have been relegated to the amateur ranks. Other nearby Serie A teams are Unione Sportiva Città di Palermo and Calcio Catania, both in Sicily, Cagliari Calcio in Sardinia, and Società Sportiva Calcio Napoli in Naples. When there's a match

on, go to the ground to pick up a ticket or head to the local bar for a couple of entertaining hours.

Hiking

Hiking is a brilliant way to experience Calabria's wonderful national parks first-hand, and spring and autumn are the optimum times to take a hike. All the national parks have trails, although, unlike in the rest of Italy, these are often not marked, signposted or

Sport and leisure

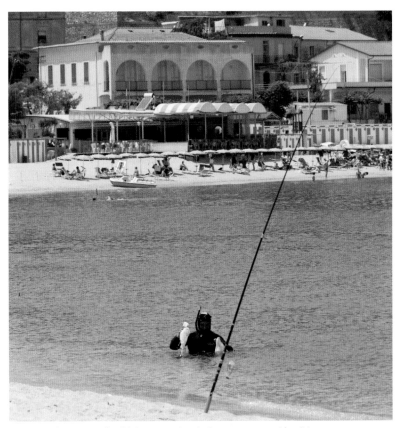

The crystal-clear waters of Calabria, as seen here in Soverato, are good for diving

Sport and leisure

mapped, so it's best to go with a guide. The local Pro Loco tourist offices have information on hiking, although it's generally only in Italian, such as the helpful brochure *A Piedi in Sila Grande*. They should also have a list of professional guides working in the area, and there are several good tour companies in Calabria offering guided walks throughout the region. Itineraries range from a couple of hours to multi-day hikes with guides. Besides the wonderful, perfumed air of the Mediterranean mountains, you'll also get to enjoy spotting rare fauna and flora. For instance, in Parco Nazionale della Sila alone, there are 31 themed nature itineraries through the provinces

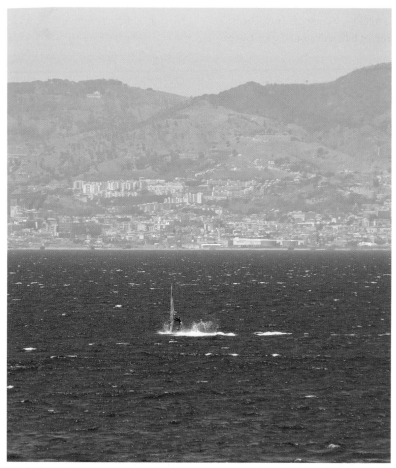

Windsurfing is a popular sport on the southern coast

of Catanzaro, Crotone and Cosenza. Nothing other than the usual gear is needed: a good map, compass, decent hiking shoes, rucksack, water, snacks and protective rain gear.

Horse riding

Camigliatello is the spot to go outside the winter months as it has a riding school. There is good riding to be had in the thick, canopied forests, across rolling hills and around cobalt lakes.

Sailing

For sailors – or potential sailors – there is everything available from catamaran classes to yacht hire. Many of the beach clubs (lidos) have windsurfing equipment for hire as well as catamarans, and the busier summer destinations such as Tropea have sailing schools that mainly rent out Hobie Cats. The seas are generally safe for beginners but fun enough for intermediate sailors. Yachts can be hired with or without crews, mainly on the west coast. The sailing around the UNESCO World Heritage-listed volcanic Isole Eolie (Aeolian Islands) is understandably popular, as is nearby Sicily as a sailing destination. Costs are from around €1,800 per week for a 9m (30ft) yacht without skipper.

Skiing

While most Italians will tell you that the main skiing action in Italy is in the north, there are some ski resorts in Calabria. They're most suitable for beginners and intermediates, with the tiny resort town of Camigliatello having the finest facilities. The slopes are best from January to March, and the cross-country skiing through the magnificent forests is recommended. Camigliatello is also a good choice because when the promised snow fails to come there are interesting walks and drives to do, a few quality restaurants, and shops selling mouthwatering local produce and wines to warm the soul until the snow falls.

Windsurfing and kitesurfing

Windsurfing and kitesurfing are very popular in Calabria, especially in the Reggio di Calabria region and the southern coast. Both areas are best suited to intermediate and advanced surfers. Winds of up to 10 knots can be expected, and during summer the consistent Borea winds are around 18–25 knots. Summer here also means no wetsuit, while during the winter months a normal full-length wetsuit will suffice in water temperatures of around 16°C (61°F). The beaches in Calabria are generally sandy or of fine pebbles, so there is little in the way of water hazards, apart from strong currents. Crowded beaches can be a problem for kitesurfers during summer. Punta Pellaro, just south of Reggio, is a popular spot, as is Lazzaro further down the coast. Reggio itself has a great launch spot, as does Catona up the coast from the city. All are an easy drive from each other.

Children

Calabria might not offer sophisticated attractions for children – don't expect to find the sprawling theme parks of Lake Garda in the north – but the 'back to nature' aspects of the region, the mountains and the sea, offer plenty of opportunities for the young ones to enjoy the great outdoors. All children love winter fun in the mountains, while the watersports and opportunities to play with other children at the lidos can keep children happy for a week or so.

As a bonus, Italians love children, and little ones are well provided for in the popular holiday resorts of the region. Cafés and restaurants in Calabria are well used to catering for children and generally welcome them with open arms. Babies in particular are adored, so don't be surprised if the grandmotherly owner of a restaurant plucks your newborn out of your arms and wanders around the room with your offspring showing him or her off to the other cooing customers. On the plus side, you can always count on a waitress to take a crying baby off your hands and keep the little one amused for ten minutes while you finish your meal in peace.

The more popular restaurants in holiday spots will have long children's menus, and, when they don't, a couple of scoops of gelato can keep even the most hyperactive child (and adult!) entertained for a few minutes. On a practical note, most eateries have high chairs, and many casual alfresco places at beach resorts are installing playgrounds with plastic equipment.

If visiting in summer, you'll find that you're not alone in bringing the little ones to the beach. The annual summer August holiday is family time for all Italians and the lidos (with all their recreational facilities) are the place to settle in for the day. Apart from facilities such as food and drink, there are often playgrounds, games such as table football (also called *foosball*, a local favourite) and mini-golf, and watersports equipment for hire. One thing to be careful of is the heat of the day in Calabria – be sure to take plenty of sunblock, hats, and lots of water for the children.

Winter-sports facilities mainly centre around cross-country skiing, but there are some slopes at Camigliatello that are fun for the kids, with toboggans and sleds for hire. The mountains also make a great area for families to explore in the warmer months, with plenty of paths, the occasional rowing boat for hire and wonderful picnic spots around the lakes in Sila National Park.

Some of the east-coast towns that cater for holidaying Italian families also boast bowling alleys and water parks, although, once again, these are fairly primitive compared to those in the rest of Italy. The bowling alleys will often have a pizzeria attached so you can make an evening of it. On the downside, they're generally on the outskirts of town and are difficult to get to for those without cars. One of the best water parks is **Acquapark Odissea** at Zolfara in Rossano (*Tel: (0983) 569 323*). This and other parks tend to be open only from June to September.

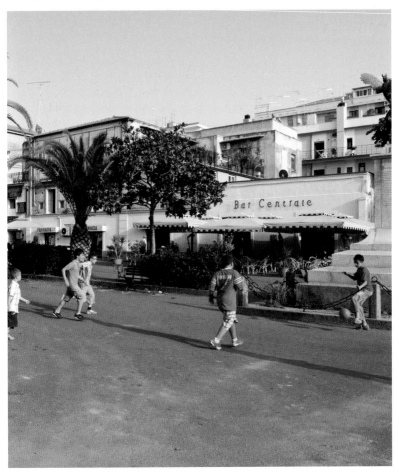

Local children love to play football wherever they can in Tropea

Essentials

Arriving and departing
By air
Calabria has two airports: at Reggio di Calabria (REG, Aeroporto dello Stretto) and at Lamezia Terme (SUF, Lamezia Terme International Airport). Both are mainly domestic, with most flights coming from Milan or Rome. Naples and Palermo in Sicily have better international links.

By land
The A3 *autostrada* from Naples goes all the way to Reggio di Calabria and is an excellent road. There are exits for all major towns along the route.

By rail
Intercity and Eurostar trains link Reggio di Calabria to Naples (four or five hours) and Rome (six to seven hours). The route is very scenic. For tickets, go to *www.ferroviedellostato.it*

By sea
Frequent ferries go across the Strait of Messina to Sicily from Reggio di Calabria and car ferries from Villa San Giovanni (*www.carontetourist.it*). The trip takes around 20 minutes.

Customs
Italian customs allow a 'reasonable amount' of alcohol and tobacco products to be brought into Italy from other EU countries. From non-EU countries, the limits are 200 cigarettes or 50 cigars, 2 litres of table wine or 1 litre of alcohol.

Electricity
Italy runs on 220V. Plugs are either European two-rounded or three-rounded pins. UK appliances will work with an adaptor.

Internet
Internet availability in Calabria is more limited than in most other parts of the country, but many towns have an Internet café. Most five-star hotels will have some form of Internet access.

Money
The currency of Italy is the euro (€), which is divided into 100 centesimi (cents). Post offices offer decent exchange rates. The usual credit and debit cards are accepted at most places, but it's good to carry cash for pizzerie and trattorie, and for tipping. ATMs (called Bankomats) are not as plentiful in Calabria as in other parts of Italy, so take advantage of them when you see them. Many ATMs work only with Italian cards, so don't panic if your card is rejected at one bank; just try another.

Opening hours
Opening hours tend to be erratic. Most shops are open 9am or 10am–noon or 1pm, and 3pm or

Essentials

4pm–7pm or even 8pm in seaside towns. Most shops are closed Monday morning and many on Wednesday afternoon. Churches are generally open 8am–noon and 3–6pm. Restaurant hours are typically noon–2pm or 3pm, and 7–10pm. Pizzerie and *enoteche* may stay open a lot later, but the kitchen will typically close at the usual time. Museums and attractions are generally closed on Mondays. Banks are usually open 9am–noon or 1pm; some may also open for an hour or two in the afternoon.

Passports and visas

EU citizens can enter Italy for an unlimited stay with a valid passport. US, Australian, Canadian and New Zealand citizens must have passports that are valid for at least three months from entry date and can stay for up to three months within a six-month period without a pre-arranged visa.

Pharmacies

Southern Italian pharmacies (*farmacie*) may not appear to have shelves bulging with stock as they do in the rest of Europe, but they are highly competent and helpful in assisting with the minor ailments that beset travellers. While it's always best to take your prescription medicine with you, Italian pharmacies will generally stock the same medicines, but often under a different brand name, with many available over the counter. For after-hours assistance, ask at your hotel for the nearest open

CONVERSION TABLE

FROM	TO	MULTIPLY BY
Inches	Centimetres	2.54
Feet	Metres	0.3048
Yards	Metres	0.9144
Miles	Kilometres	1.6090
Acres	Hectares	0.4047
Gallons	Litres	4.5460
Ounces	Grams	28.35
Pounds	Grams	453.6
Pounds	Kilograms	0.4536
Tons	Tonnes	1.0160

To convert back, for example from centimetres to inches, divide by the number in the third column.

MEN'S SUITS

UK	36	38	40	42	44	46	48
Rest of Europe	46	48	50	52	54	56	58
USA	36	38	40	42	44	46	48

DRESS SIZES

UK	8	10	12	14	16	18
France	36	38	40	42	44	46
Italy	38	40	42	44	46	48
Rest of Europe	34	36	38	40	42	44
USA	6	8	10	12	14	16

MEN'S SHIRTS

UK	14	14.5	15	15.5	16	16.5	17
Rest of Europe	36	37	38	39/40	41	42	43
USA	14	14.5	15	15.5	16	16.5	17

MEN'S SHOES

UK	7	7.5	8.5	9.5	10.5	11
Rest of Europe	41	42	43	44	45	46
USA	8	8.5	9.5	10.5	11.5	12

WOMEN'S SHOES

UK	4.5	5	5.5	6	6.5	7
Rest of Europe	38	38	39	39	40	41
USA	6	6.5	7	7.5	8	8.5

Essentials

pharmacy – they operate on a roster system.

Post

Sending postcards is cheap and generally reliable, but sending parcels overseas is expensive and risky, so it's advisable to use a courier. The post office of each village or town is generally in the centre and is always noted on local maps.

Public holidays

1 January	**New Year's Day**
6 January	**Epiphany**
March/April	**Easter Monday**
25 April	**Liberation Day**
1 May	**Labour Day**
2 June	**Republic Day**
15 August	**Feast of the Assumption**
1 November	**All Saints' Day**
8 December	**Immaculate Conception**
25 December	**Christmas Day**
26 December	**St Stephen's Day**

Smoking

Since 2005, smoking has been banned everywhere but private homes and specially designated areas. *Vietato fumare* (no smoking) signs are generally (albeit grudgingly) adhered to.

Suggested reading and media

Newspapers and periodicals in English are generally found only in holiday resort areas such as Tropea, and good paperbacks are also scarce.

Here are some Calabrian-focused titles to whet your appetite:
A Traveller in Southern Italy by H V Morton. An entertaining journey through the south by a travel writer armed with a wonderful way with the English language.
Calabrian Tales by Peter Chiarella. A compelling read, this saga neatly describes the Calabrian experience of the late 19th century.
Cucina di Calabria: Treasured Recipes and Family Traditions from Southern Italy by Mary Amabile Palmer. Authentic Calabrian recipes.
Old Calabria by Norman Douglas. Based on travels in the early 20th century, it depicts Calabria as the wild and inscrutable destination it was until only recently.

Tax

Most hotels charge 9 per cent VAT (value-added tax), while top-end hotels charge 12 per cent. Restaurants don't charge VAT but will add 10–15 per cent to the bill. If you are buying luxury items to take out of Italy, you may be eligible to receive a tax refund if you are not an EU resident. The tax can be 20 per cent, 10 per cent or 4 per cent, so it's worth looking for shops displaying the Tax Free Shopping logo. For more information visit the Global Refund website (*www.globalrefund.com*).

Telephones

Public payphones are rare in Calabria (try the main squares) and require a *carta telefonica* sold at newsstands. Italy uses the GSM mobile system; your service provider at home will be able to advise whether you can use your own mobile in Italy or not. Another option is to take an old unlocked phone and purchase a prepaid SIM card, as these are widely available and calls are cheap. All numbers beginning with *3* are mobile numbers.

To make an international call from inside Italy using an operator, dial *170*. Otherwise dial *00*, then the country code (Australia *61*, Canada *1*, Ireland *353*, New Zealand *64*, South Africa *27*, UK *44*, USA *1*), the area code (minus the first *0*) and the local number.

To telephone Italy from abroad, dial international access (usually *00*), then the country code (*39*), the area code (without the *0*) and the local number. To dial a number within Italy, always use the area code (including the *0*). The area code for Calabria is *09*, generally followed by a two-digit code for the province.

Time

Italy's time zone is Central European (GMT + 1). Daylight saving is from the end of March to the end of September. Italy is one hour ahead of the UK, six hours ahead of the East Coast USA, one hour behind Pretoria, South Africa, ten hours behind Sydney, and twelve hours behind Auckland.

Toilets

Your best bet on the *autostrade* are the Autogrill stops, where they clean the toilets regularly. In towns and villages,

the local café is a good bet, but at least buy a coffee. Always carry some tissues.

Travellers with disabilities

Facilities for travellers with disabilities in Italy are generally poor but slowly improving. The situation in Calabria, however, lags behind the rest of the country. Cobbled streets, limited parking and a lack of ramps, along with seemingly never-ending road and building works, compound the problem. Non-profit **Accessible Italy** (*www. accessibleitaly.com*) is a great resource.

Small shops such as this one in Reggio always stock telephone cards

Language

Calabrians who deal with travellers regularly will generally speak some English, but it is far less common in Calabria to meet people on the street fluent in the language than it is in the rest of Italy, so it helps to learn some basic Italian and buy a phrasebook. As in the rest of Italy, locals' faces light up when you at least begin a sentence with *Buon giorno* (Good day).

PRONUNCIATION

c and cc = ch if before e and i, as in 'cheap', otherwise like a k

ch = before e and i, is hard, like a k

g and gg = soft, like a j, if before e and i, as in 'George'

gh = hard, as in 'gorge'

g = soft, rolling sound with the g almost silent

gn = ny, as in 'canyon'

gl = ll, as in 'medallion'

q = kw, as in 'quick'

sc = soft before an e or an i, as in 'shed'

sch = hard, as in 'skip'

z = ts except when it starts a word, then ds

EVERYDAY EXPRESSIONS

English	Italian
Hello	**Ciao**
Goodbye	**Arrivederci**
Good morning	**Buon giorno**
Good afternoon	**Buona sera**
Good evening	**Buona sera**
Goodnight	**Buona notte**
Please	**Per favore**
Thank you	**Grazie**
You're welcome	**Prego**
I'm sorry	**Mi dispiace**
I don't understand	**Non capisco**
Excuse me (to get past someone)	**Scusi/Permesso**
Yes	**Sì**
No	**No**
OK	**Va bene**
Go away!	**Va via!**
Cheers!	**Salute!**
At what time...?	**A che ora...?**
Do you speak English?	**Parla inglese?**
I don't speak Italian	**Non parlo italiano**
Where is...?	**Dove...?**
There is/are...	**C'è/Ci sono...**
There is/are not...	**Non c'è/Non ci sono...**
I want...	**Voglio...**
I would like...	**Vorrei...**
How much?	**Quanto?**
The bill, please	**Il conto, per favore**
Big/little	**Grande/piccolo**
Hot/cold	**Caldo/freddo**
Open/closed	**Aperto/chiuso**
Right/left	**Destra/sinistra**

Good/bad	**Buono/cattivo**	
Fast/slow	**Presto/lento**	
Much/little	**Molto/poco**	
Expensive/cheap	**Caro/economico**	
Money	**Soldi**	
Toilet	**La toilette/**	
	Il gabinetto	
Men's toilet	**Signori**	
Women's toilet	**Signore/Dame**	
Today	**Oggi**	
Yesterday	**Ieri**	
Tomorrow	**Domani**	
What is the time?	**Che ore sono?**	

NUMBERS

1	**Uno**
2	**Due**
3	**Tre**
4	**Quattro**
5	**Cinque**
6	**Sei**
7	**Sette**
8	**Otto**
9	**Nove**
10	**Dieci**
11	**Undici**
12	**Dodici**
13	**Tredici**
14	**Quattordici**
15	**Quindici**
16	**Sedici**
17	**Diciassette**
18	**Diciotto**
19	**Diciannove**
20	**Venti**
21	**Ventuno**
22	**Ventidue**
30	**Trenta**
40	**Quaranta**
50	**Cinquanta**
60	**Sessanta**
70	**Settanta**
80	**Ottanta**
90	**Novanta**
100	**Cento**
200	**Duecento**
500	**Cinquecento**
1,000	**Mille**

DAYS OF THE WEEK

Monday	**Lunedì**
Tuesday	**Martedì**
Wednesday	**Mercoledì**
Thursday	**Giovedì**
Friday	**Venerdì**
Saturday	**Sabato**
Sunday	**Domenica**

MONTHS OF THE YEAR

January	**Gennaio**
February	**Febbraio**
March	**Marzo**
April	**Aprile**
May	**Maggio**
June	**Giugno**
July	**Luglio**
August	**Agosto**
September	**Settembre**
October	**Ottobre**
November	**Novembre**
December	**Dicembre**

Emergencies

Medical services

If you need non-urgent medical treatment, nearly every village has a local doctor (*medico*), and your hotel will generally have an English-speaking doctor that it uses. If you need to visit the casualty ward of a hospital, always ask for the nearest one that's likely to have the shortest waiting time. If you need dental work, once again ask your hotel for a list of local dentists (*dentisti*). If you wear glasses or contact lenses, take a copy of your prescription to save an optometrist (*ottico*) having to retest your eyes in the event of your losing or damaging your lenses. Note that, while the EU and many other countries (such as Australia) have a reciprocal arrangement with Italy on emergency medical care, this does not generally cover dental or optical needs.

Insurance

While your own country might have emergency medical cover arrangements with Italy, it's always a good idea (and good for peace of mind) to have insurance to cover against theft or loss of luggage as well as illness or injury. Note that a general policy might not cover so-called dangerous sports such as kitesurfing and skiing.

Health risks

The most common health concerns for visitors to Calabria are sunburn and diarrhoea. The former can be avoided by the use of sunblock and a decent wide-brimmed hat, while the risk of the latter is reduced by drinking only bottled water and avoiding raw or undercooked seafood or meat and raw fruits that you haven't peeled yourself. Most bouts of travellers' diarrhoea pass within a few days. If yours doesn't, seek medical help.

Police, safety and crime

Pickpockets and purse-snatchers are not as common in Calabria as in other more touristy destinations in Italy, but car thieves are still on the job here. If you absolutely have to leave valuables in the car, be sure to keep them out of sight. Despite what you might have read, the local Mafia doesn't bother tourists. The police are extremely visible and should be able to help if you have a problem. Don't expect many to speak any English, though.

Embassies and consulates

The following national representative offices are those located closest to Calabria:

Australia *Via Antonio Bosio 5, 00161 Rome. Tel: (06) 852 721.*

Canada *Via Zara 30, 00198 Rome. Tel: (06) 854 442 912.*

New Zealand *Via Clitunno 44, 00198 Rome. Tel: (06) 853 7501.*

South Africa *Via Tanaro 14, 00198 Rome. Tel: (06) 852 541.*

UK *Via XX Settembre, 00187 Rome. Tel: (06) 422 000 01.*

USA *Piazza della Repubblica, 80122 Naples. Tel: (08) 158 381 11.*

A highway patrolman in Reggio

Directory

Accommodation price guide

Prices of accommodation are based on a double room per night for two people sharing, with breakfast.

★	up to €80
★★	€80–130
★★★	€130–200
★★★★	over €200

Eating out price guide

Prices are based on an average three-course meal for one, without drinks.

★	up to €25
★★	€25–50
★★★	€50–70
★★★★	over €70

Calabrian restaurants, including trattorie, tend to open for lunch from noon until 2.30pm (occasionally 11.30am–3pm). Dinner is usually served from 8pm until 10.30pm, although in tourist areas they may open at 7–7.30pm for foreigners, and stay open later for Italian tourists.

Enoteche and *osterie* will sometimes open only in the evenings for drinks and for dinner. Be aware that in small villages some places will close on a whim if there isn't anybody around.

REGGIO DI CALABRIA PROVINCE

Gerace

ACCOMMODATION

La Casa di Gianna ★★
Tucked away on a side street in the heart of town, this converted residence has rather grand pretensions and mostly succeeds in delivering. While the décor is a medley of 20th-century interior design, old-fashioned touches abound, but the service is a shaky affair.
Via Paolo Frascà 4.
Tel: (0964) 355 024/018.
www.lacasadigianna.it

Il Giardino di Gerace ★★
This charming B&B with an attractive garden makes a cheaper (and more hospitable) alternative to La Casa di Gianna (*see below*) if there are rooms available. It's tricky to locate, so call ahead or ask the locals.
Villa Fanfani 8.
Tel: (0964) 356 732.

EATING OUT

La Terrazza ★
Hearty local food cooked with care on a covered terrace with lovely views. The antipasti and anything made in-house at this long-established, family-run restaurant are delicious.
Via Nazionale.
Tel: (0964) 356 739.

La Casa di Gianna ★★★
An elegant restaurant located in a series of simple rooms with old-fashioned service and regional cuisine. The quality of food can be hit and miss, but there is little choice in town, and when it's good it's superb.
Via Paolo Frascà 4.

Tel: (0964) 355 024/018.
www.lacasadigianna.it

ENTERTAINMENT

Gerace has a lively calendar of festivals for a small village, but it has little in the way of evening entertainment, and the streets are quiet after dark. There are a couple of cafés on the two main squares and the occasional concert in one of the churches. Gerace is at its liveliest during summer.

Reggio di Calabria
ACCOMMODATION
L'Attico ★

The young managers of this clean, comfortable B&B will happily steer you in the direction of the city's best entertainment and nightlife. Rooms have large sun terraces with street views. Breakfast is at a nearby café.
Via Demetrio Tripepi 149.
Tel: 320 564 3251.
www.welcometorc.it
B&B Delfina ★
This centrally located B&B has spacious, light and airy, simply decorated rooms with

balconies. There's Internet access, and the hospitable owners will ensure you make the most of your stay.
Via Crocefisso 58.
Tel: (0965) 890 977.
www.bb-delfina.com
Bed & Breakfast Reggio ★
This excellent organisation of about a dozen B&Bs has one website where you can look at the properties and make bookings. The B&Bs in Reggio are often better value than the hotels and have free Internet access and other extras.
Tel: 334 161 3905.
www.bb-reggio.it
Continental Hotel ★★
While it's not so handily located, this hotel is a clean, reasonably well-equipped choice for this price range and may be your only option if there's a concert or event on in town during your stay.
Via Florio 10.
Tel: (0965) 249 90.
www.hotelcontinentalrc.it
Hotel Lungomare ★★
Opened in 2002 in a delightful old building on the seafront promenade (rooms with

sea view come at a premium), this is a great mid-range choice. Rooms are clean, and the staff are friendly.
Viale Zerbi 13b.
Tel: (0965) 204 86.
www.hotellungomare.rc.it
Hotel Palace Masoanri's ★★
Opposite the Grand Hotel Excelsior (see p160) and close to the archaeological museum, this clean, decent mid-range hotel isn't as flashy as its neighbour across the road but it's good value and is handily placed for sightseeing and shopping.
Via Vittorio Veneto 95.
Tel: (0965) 264 33.
www.montesanohotels.it
Possidonea 28 ★★
This chic B&B is beautifully decorated with Moroccan furnishings and vibrantly coloured walls (all rooms are different) and has a relaxing feel about it. It's in a great location, and the young owners are very accommodating.
Via Possidonea 28.
Tel: 339 410 4990/
347 945 9210.
www.possidonea28.it

Grand Hotel Excelsior ★★★

The best hotel in town, this is a well-appointed property with spacious, comfortable rooms and a great position adjacent to the National Magna Graecia Archaeological Museum. The rooftop restaurant and breakfast room have fantastic views – be sure to ask for a room with a view as well.

Via Vittorio Veneto 66.
Tel: (0965) 812 211.
www.montesanohotels.it

EATING OUT

Il Fiore del Cappero ★★

Seafood doesn't get any better in Reggio than at this elegant restaurant, the city's best. Expect highly creative cuisine (try their house antipasto seafood plate), a superb wine list and wonderful friendly service courtesy of a couple of local brothers. A local favourite, this is a good choice for either a casual lunch or slightly more formal dinner.

Via Zaleuco 7.
Tel: (0965) 209 55. Email:
ilfioredelcappero@libero.it

La Forchetta d'Oro ★★

By no means Calabria's best, but this is a good choice for Italian pasta and meat standards, as well as fresh local fish and Calabrian specialities, such as the 'nduja.

Via Bixio 5.
Tel: (0965) 896 048.

Ristorante Il Ducale ★★

With wonderful seafront views this elegant restaurant unsurprisingly focuses much of its menu on seafood and fish, including swordfish and squid. The décor has hints of the Baroque about it, which all adds to the atmosphere.

Corso Vittorio Emanuele III 13.
Tel: (0965) 891 520.

Via Veneto ★★

This massive, fun, buzzy restaurant is one of the most popular in town. Local groups come here and settle in for a night of enormous servings of *fritto misto* (mixed fried specialities), the buffet antipasti and massive fresh pizzas. Arrive with a healthy appetite. Great value.

Via Veneto 64.
Tel: (0965) 810 306.

Baylik ★★★

Ignore the odd combination of outdoor furniture and elegant linen table settings inside, and instead focus on the port views, fresh seafood and fine pastas. This long-standing favourite (opened in 1950) may not be as popular as it once was, but it's definitely still worth a try.

Vico Leone 1.
Tel: (0965) 486 24.

ENTERTAINMENT

B'Art

This stylish and very busy café-bar in the same building as the theatre and art gallery is a good spot for a glass of something in the evening or a nightcap after a show.

Corso Giuseppe Garibaldi 325.
Tel: (0965) 332 908.
www.bartcafe.com

La Brace

La Brace is a very popular and lively local wine bar and trattoria, with excellent local wines.

Viale Rosselli 18.
Tel: (0965) 331 434.

Gelateria Cesare

Any walk along the waterfront of Reggio is

not complete without working your way through one of the sweet delights from this famous *gelateria* – in operation for over 50 years.
Piazza Indipendenza.
www.gelateriacesare.it

Le Rose al Bicchiere
This cosy wine bar heats up later at night, when locals head here for meat, cheeses and DOC wines. On weekend afternoons they offer high tea.
Via Demetrio Tripepi 118.
Tel: (0965) 229 56.

Teatro Francesco Cilea
Reggio's beautiful old theatre – the largest in the region – hosts a lively programme of classical music, jazz and pop concerts, theatre, opera, ballet and dance.
Corso Giuseppe Garibaldi.
Tel: (0965) 895 162. www.
teatrofrancescocilea.it

Sport and leisure
Giro Calabria
This local tour company offers a wide range of half- and full-day tours around Calabria and Sicily, including excursions to Pizzo and Tropea, Locri and Gerace, Pentedattilo, Saline and the Aspromonte National Park, and across to Etna, Alcantara and Taormina. Hotel pickup and drop-off.
Tel: 334 161 3905.
www.girocalabria.it

Reggio surrounds
Accommodation
B&B Villa Virginia ★★
This beautiful B&B, 13km (8 miles) south of Reggio, can also be rented out as an entire villa and is ideal for families who want to be close to the beach. The area is a popular windsurfing spot.
Via Vico D'Angelo, Bocale II. Tel: (0965) 331 600.
www.villavirginia.it

Altafiumara Resort & Spa ★★★★
A swish resort hotel located between Villa San Giovanni and Scilla (11km/6¾ miles from Reggio di Calabria), parklands and gardens make it a unique property in this region. There is a variety of room styles and sizes on offer, as well as an excellent spa.
Santa Trada di Cannitello, Villa San Giovanni.
Tel: (0965) 759 804.
www.altafiumarahotel.it

Scilla
Accommodation
Hotel U Bais ★★
The hotel's name comes from the Italian word for 'well balanced' or 'fair' (*baisate*) and the hotel is indeed a good balance of position (it's just behind the waterfront), price and amenities. The rooms have enchanting names such as Sognatrice ('Woman Dreamer'). Make sure to book a room with a balcony, as interior rooms are dark.
Via Nazionale 65.
Tel: (0965) 704 300.
www.hotelubais.it

Principe di Scilla ★★★★
This elegant, beautifully decorated hotel is the loveliest in town and oozes atmosphere. The rooms are individually decorated and suite 103, the Regina Paola Ruffo di Calabria, is exquisite.
Via Grotte 2.
Tel: (0965) 704 324.
www.hotelubais.it

Eating out
There are a number of popular restaurants, bars

and cafés along the waterfront. Make a booking for weekend evenings, when tables are taken early and places seem to stay full until closing.

Grotta Azzurra ★★

Once you've overlooked the somewhat naff nautical theme (fishing nets hanging from the ceiling and so forth), you'll find this beachfront restaurant is full of locals, here to sample the no-nonsense, honest seafood dishes, such as the fantastic *gnocchetti* pasta and scampi in a tomato sauce. The *antipasto misto* is also a treat.
Lungomare.
Tel: (0965) 754 889.

Il Pirata ★★★

On the other side of the town, away from the Lungomare (seafront roadway), this restaurant has a wonderful position, with tables on a deck right over the water where you can watch the swordfish boats bring in their catch – soon to be destined for the tables here. Great seafood and service.

Via Grotte 22.
Tel: (0965) 704 292.

ENTERTAINMENT

There are several bars along the Lungomare that are lively in summer, as well as a couple of casual bar-cafés set up on the waterfront.

SPORT AND LEISURE

In Scilla, activities focus on the wonderful waterfront, and the beach gets crowded in summer. The lidos along the Lungomare such as Lido Nettuno and Lido Paradiso have all kinds of flotation and propulsion devices for hire.

Stilo

ACCOMMODATION

Hotel San Giorgio ★★★

Located in a 17th-century former cardinal's palace, this hotel has a marvellous setting of which the cardinal would certainly approve today. Wonderful ambience, fantastic views and decent food. Open April–September.
Via Citareli 8.
Tel: (0964) 775 047.

EATING OUT

Apart from the restaurant at the San Giorgio hotel, these are mainly cafés and *gelaterie*.

VIBO VALENTIA PROVINCE

Pizzo

ACCOMMODATION

Casa Armonia B&B ★

Located in the heart of Pizzo's historic centre, this B&B has a homely, endearing feel. The 18th-century building features a large terrace, and the owner speaks English.
Via Armonia 9.
Tel: 339 374 3731.
www.casaarmonia.com

Hotel Marinella ★

This modern three-star hotel and restaurant located down the beach from the historic centre has decent-sized rooms with large terraces.
Via Riviera Prangi.
Tel: (0963) 534 860.
www.hotelmarinella.info

EATING OUT

Le Castellane ★★

Your best bet on the rather touristy main square, this tastefully decorated restaurant delivers superb local cuisine, along with a good wine list and friendly, professional service.

Piazza della Repubblica. Tel: (0963) 532 551.

La Lamia ★★

A traditional restaurant and wine bar with sophisticated cuisine that defies the casual setting. Some great wines on offer, too.

Largo Volcano 3. Tel: 328 777 4281.

Toscano ★★

This petite and intimate trattoria and pizzeria takes its cuisine seriously, with a fine short menu featuring Italian classics plus a few Calabrian specialities.

Via B Musolino 14/16. Tel: (0963) 534 162.

ENTERTAINMENT

Entertainment in Pizzo is based around the main square, Piazza della Repubblica, where in summer beer matches gelato sale for sale. Any of the cafés are fine for a brew, as are any of the *gelaterie* for the famous tartufo – chocolate and hazelnut gelato sprinkled with cocoa powder and with a chocolate fudge or sauce centre.

Tropea

ACCOMMODATION

Residenza Il Barone ★★

Housed in a wonderful historic building in the old centre, this all-suites boutique hotel is stunning – stylish, contemporary and minimalist, with all mod cons for those who want to experience the cobbled streets without forgoing a little luxury to do it. The views from the terrace, where you can take breakfast or a drink, are breathtaking.

Largo Barone. Tel: (0963) 607 181/340 309 8197. www.residenzailbarone.it

Villa Giada ★★

Right down next to the beach is Villa Giada, with nine comfortable double and triple rooms set among some lovely gardens.

Via Marina del Convento. Tel: (0963) 607 050. www. villagiadatropea.com

Il Convento ★★★

Located right on the cliff face, these stylish apartments have some of the best views in town. There's one that's perfect for a couple (Sole) and another (Luna), with two bedrooms and two bathrooms, that is great for a family or group of friends.

Via Abate Sergio 10. Tel: 347 509 0576. www.ilconvento.com

EATING OUT

Vecchio Forno ★

This massively popular pizzeria sees customers lining up for an outside table every evening during summer. The reason? It's simple, inexpensive and fuss-free. Takeaway available.

Via Caviano. Tel: 347 311 2416.

Da Cecè ★★

A local favourite and Tropea's best, this elegant family-run restaurant has garnered its reputation by doing regional specialities exceedingly well. Try their *spaghetti con cipolla* (local sweet onions) or *antipasto di mare* (seafood antipasto). Friendly service and well-chosen wines. Book

in summer for the front alfresco terrace.
Largo Toraldo Grimaldi. Tel: (0963) 603 219.

Hosteria Italiana ★★

A nice break from the usual terraced eateries, this chic wine bar and restaurant takes a spin on local favourites while hip music plays in the background.
Via Boiano Dardano. Tel: (0963) 626 12.

La Munizione ★★

A good place for a drink in summer on the terrace, this restaurant also has a good menu, with Calabrian classics including excellent fresh fish.
Largo Duomo 12. Tel: 347 808 0511.

Il Normanno ★★

With lovely views of the valley behind town and the marina below, the shady terrace at this popular restaurant is a good place to sit. While the view makes the slow service a little more palatable, the food itself (local favourites and pizza) is fine. Try the menu of the day.
Largo Duomo. Tel: (0963) 603 240.

Le Volpi e L'Uva ★★

A good, honest little *osteria* (wine bar) boasting a short but excellent menu. Expect generous servings of pasta and hearty local specialities. They do an enormous *antipasto di mare* (seafood antipasto). Friendly staff.
Via Garibaldi 11. Tel: (0963) 619 00.

ENTERTAINMENT

In the main part of town, entertainment mainly consists of hanging out in the shade by day, eating gelato and wondering if it's not too early to order a beer! Come sunset, everyone is eating their gelato on the terrace overlooking the sea, or drinking beer (yep, you've guessed it – on the terrace overlooking the sea!).

SPORT AND LEISURE

Briatico Eolie

Departing from Tropea port most afternoons during the summer, the *Ischiamar II* offers 'Stromboli by night' cruises across to the Aeolian Islands. If you're lucky enough to catch the volcano erupting, it's a memorable experience.
Tel: port (0963) 395 865, boat 340 060 6382.

Cooking classes

Learn how to cook authentic local specialities with Marianna in her charming country home in the Tropea hills, a few minutes from town, and then enjoy eating the meal you've cooked washed down with local wine. Hotel pickup and drop-off.
Tel: (0963) 61 952/329 326 3413.
www.initalytours.com

CST Tropea

This excellent tour company and travel agency organises walking, trekking and mountain-biking excursions, diving, windsurfing and catamaranning, boat trips from Tropea to Capo Vaticano, 'Stromboli by night' tours, day trips to Reggio, airport transfers and car hire.
Largo San Michele 7. Tel: (0963) 611 78/339 760 1124.
www.csttropea.it

Moonlight Bike

Mountain-biking

excursions into nearby mountains and along country tracks, covering anything from half-day excursions of 30km (18½ miles) to full-day tours of 75km (47 miles), starting at €30.

La Pineta, Via Marina Vescovado.
Tel: (0963) 760 1124.
www.velamoonlight.com

Shark Bay Water Sports
On La Grazia beach, Shark Bay hires out jet-skis, canoes and pedal boats, and offers waterskiing and banana-boating, as well as boat excursions.

La Grazia, Parghelia (near Tropea Port).
Tel: 329 424 6671/ 347 000 1843.
www.tropeanautica.com

Stromboli Express
Departing from Tropea's port most days during the summer, this air-conditioned boat offers excursions to the Aeolian Islands, including harbour visits and shopping trips, and in the evening a glimpse of the volcano island of Stromboli erupting.

Comerci Navigazione, Tropea Port.
Tel: port (0963) 395 849,
boat 348 609 1917.
www.comerci.it

Trekking
The Antico Sentiero Association organises themed full-day nature, history and gastronomy walks through the mountains and villages surrounding Tropea, taking in castle ruins, creeks and waterfalls and often involving a visit to a Calabrian farm for lunch. Hotel pickup and drop-off.

Tel: 338 673 4943.
www.tropeatrekking.it

Tropea surrounds
ACCOMMODATION
Capo Vaticano Beach Resort ★★★
A beautiful, stylish property that opened in 2008, its chic design is one that doesn't detract from the notion that you're here to relax, not live in a modern art museum. Highlights are the pool and beach area and the hotel's cuisine.

Località Tono, Capo Vaticano.
Tel: (0963) 665 760.
www.hotelphilosophy.com

Hotel Panta Rei ★★★★
A gorgeous, exclusive property set about 5km (3 miles) from Tropea, this hotel has rooms with a refined ambience and wonderful views. The pool and beach areas are private.

Località Marina di San Nicola, Parghelia.
Tel: (0963) 601 865.
www.hotelpantarei.com

Porto Pirgos ★★★★
Another great property about 5km (3 miles) from Tropea, with everything you need for a relaxing stay: lovely rooms with private terraces, a swimming pool, a private beach and tennis court, and a colonnaded terrace restaurant to watch the sunset from.

Località Marina di Bordila SS522, Parghelia.
Tel: (0963) 600 351.
www.portopirgos.com

EATING OUT
If you stay at these properties, you'll probably eat in-house, as many offer full or half board. Alternatively, you can drive or take a taxi ride into Tropea (*see the restaurant reviews on the previous pages*).

Vibo Valentia
ACCOMMODATION
Vecchia Vibo Hotel ★★
Well located for explorations of the old town, this hotel is elegant in a modern classical style and extremely comfortable. They have parking, and the staff are very helpful.
Via G Murat-Scrimbia.
Tel: (0963) 430 46/412 41.
www.hotelvecchiavibo.com

San Leonardo Resort ★★★★
A luxurious hotel overlooking the harbour. Each room has a terrace and the outdoor pool has spectacular views. There's also a fitness centre and a therapy centre for the treatment of aches and pains.
SS 18 km 434.
Tel: (0963) 577 317. www.sanleonardoresort.com

EATING OUT
L'Approdo ★★★
Down at the marina, this lovely restaurant lives up to its reputation as having the best cuisine in the area – and the best seafood. The kitchen delivers Calabrian classics and inventive dishes with equal ease.
Via Roma 22.
Tel: (0963) 572 640.
www.lapprodo.com

La Locanda Daffina ★★★★
While the food here can be hit and miss and its inclusion in the Michelin guide is something to ponder, it occasionally lives up to the promise of the very elegant interior.
Via Murat 2.
Tel: (0963) 472 669.
www.lalocandadaffina.it

SPORT AND LEISURE
Briatico Eolie
Departing from Vibo Marina most afternoons during summer months, the *Ischiamar II* offers 'Stromboli by night' cruises to the Aeolian Islands (*see p164 for details*).
Tel: port (0963) 395 865, boat 340 060 6382.

Stromboli Express
Also departing from Vibo Marina most days in summer, this air-conditioned boat offers excursions to the Aeolian Islands (*see p165 for details*).
Comerci Navigazione, Tropea Port.
Tel: port (0963) 395 849, boat 348 609 1917.
www.comerci.it

CATANZARO PROVINCE
Catanzaro
ACCOMMODATION
Most travellers choose not to stay in Catanzaro city overnight, preferring to use the waterfront Catanzaro Lido as a base and driving up to the old town for a look.

Il Cedro Bed & Breakfast ★
Owned by a lovely young multilingual couple (he Italian, she American, and they speak Spanish and French), this hospitable B&B is a good base for exploring the city and surrounding area. There is satellite TV and free Internet access, and your hosts will go out of their way to ensure you enjoy every minute of your stay.
Viale Isonzo 310.
Tel: 328 973 0305.
http://ilcedro.wordpress.com

San Giuseppe Hotel ★★
It doesn't have a whole lot of character, but this

clean, no-nonsense hotel makes a perfectly adequate base for exploring the old town. The simply decorated rooms have TV, Internet access and minibar.
Salita Piazza Roma 7.
Tel: (0961) 726 172.
www.sangiuseppehotel.it

EATING OUT
La Vecchia Posta ★
This casual trattoria dishes up decent, honest food including some hearty regional specialities and good house wines from the area, so good that locals have been known to come for the wine alone.
Via degli Angioni 81.
Tel: 330 815 711.
Le Brace ★★
Le Brace is a large restaurant that deftly handles both local meat and fish specialities.
Via Melito Porto Salvo 102. Tel: (0961) 313 40.

ENTERTAINMENT
Teatro Politeama
This wonderfully designed theatre is a world-class venue for drama and music, with many orchestras from

abroad playing here.
Via Jannoni.
Tel: (0961) 501 807. www. politeamacatanzaro.net

Catanzaro Lido
ACCOMMODATION
Hotel Palace ★★★
The unusual mix of modern and period décor at this elegant hotel might irk some, but its location on the waterfront can't be beaten. It offers a private beach, bike rental, Internet access and free parking.
Via Lungomare 221.
Tel: (0961) 318 00.
www.hotel-palace.it

EATING OUT
Catanzaro is not short of eateries – there are numerous trattorie and pizzerie (several set in gardens) along the waterfront, oodles of *gelaterie* and countless café-bars – there's just nothing that is outstanding, and many present the same unadventurous menus.

SPORT AND LEISURE
Lido Holiday Agency
This popular local tour company and travel

agency offers day trips to Pizzo, Tropea, Scilla, Reggio di Calabria, the Sila mountains and more, as well as private guided visits to the markets and local sights. Contact them in advance of your trip to organise an English-speaking guide. They can also find you accommodation and organise airport transfers.
Via Nicea 3.
Tel: (0961) 333 44.
www.lidoholiday.it

COSENZA PROVINCE
Altomonte
ACCOMMODATION
Il Castello di Altomonte ★★
This 11-room five-star *albergo* in an elegant old stone palazzo, now owned by a former Italian politician turned author, once belonged to the family of the Queen of the Netherlands. Guests can sleep in the rather regal canopied bed in the suite the queen stayed in when she visited.
Piazza Castello 6.
Tel: (0981) 948 933.
www.altomonte.it

Hotel Barbieri ★★
A clean, pleasant hotel
with a variety of rooms,
a swimming pool and
a well-regarded
restaurant.
*Via Italo Barbieri 30.
Tel: (0981) 948 072.
www.barbierigroup.it*

EATING OUT
**Ristorante Il Castello di
Altomonte ★★**
While the dining room
is stunning, the food is
up to the task. Expect
highly refined (and often
creative) regional dishes
that are made from the
freshest local ingredients.
The award-winning
olive oils are sublime,
and the restaurant's
wine list is equally
impressive.
*Piazza Castello 6.
Tel: (0981) 948 933.
www.altomonte.it*

Amantea
ACCOMMODATION
Hotel Le Clarisse ★★
The hotel in this grand
old palace boasts large,
delightful rooms with
high ceilings and
spectacular views of
the coast, and a
lovely garden. The whole

place has oodles of
atmosphere, and the
hospitable owners are
equally charming.
The highly regarded
restaurant makes a night
or two here even more
appealing.
*Via Indipendenza 27.
Tel: (0982) 420 33. www.
palazzodelleclarisse.com*

EATING OUT
**Ristorante Due
Bicchieri ★★**
A fantastic
neighbourhood *enoteca*,
with excellent local
cheese and salami plates,
generously sized rustic
pastas and perfect pizzas.
There's a wonderful wine
list, and you can also buy
wines to take away –
which is highly
recommended!
*Via Dogana 92/94.
Tel: (0982) 424 409.*
**Ristorante Le
Clarisse ★★★**
An elegant restaurant
that's easily the best in
the region, with a menu
boasting creative dishes
such as pasta with sweet
rocket and strawberries,
and a well-chosen
wine list. Reserve a table
in advance, especially

at weekends, when
Italian families come
from far and wide to
dine here.
*Via Indipendenza 27.
Tel: (0982) 420 33. www.
palazzodelleclarisse.com*

Belvedere Marittimo
EATING OUT
**Ristorante Sabbia
d'Oro ★★**
Located between
Diamante and Belvedere
Marittimo, this
restaurant has built its
well-deserved reputation
on fresh seafood and
the use of hot chillies
in some of its dishes.
You must try the
gnocchetti Sabbia d'Oro
or the chilli-crusted
swordfish.
*Via Piano delle Donne 1.
Tel: (0985) 884 56.*

**Camigliatello and Sila
National Park**
ACCOMMODATION
**Hotel Aquila &
Edelweiss ★★**
This is a charming,
family-owned and
family-run hotel that has
all the comforts of home.
The old-fashioned, rustic
feel extends to the
delightful restaurant,

which is home to some of the best cuisine in the area.
Viale Stazione 15.
Tel: (0984) 578 044/765.
www.
hotelaquilaedelweiss.com
Torre Camigliati ★★
You would think that an 18th-century baronial hunting lodge would be the perfect place to stay in the mountains – and it is. The gardens are beautiful, and the cosy den has an open fireplace and lots of fascinating books, making for a grand place to hang out for a few days of walking or skiing, or a spot of mushroom picking.
Parco Old Calabria.
Tel: (0984) 578 200.
www.torrecamigliati.it

Hotel Aquila & Edelweiss ★★
It's no secret that the best traditional cooking in town is here. Chef Angela Valente knows all the secrets of the mountains. Soups such as her courgette, chick pea or borlotti bean are the stuff

of legend, as is any pasta that's handmade that day, such as her ravioli.
Viale Stazione 15.
Tel: (0984) 578 044/765.
www.
hotelaquilaedelweiss.com
La Tavernetta ★★
What was once a rustic old tavern has been transformed into the most contemporary of Sila restaurants. Bold colours adorn the walls, and bold flavours are evident on the plates. What remains of the old is respect for fresh local ingredients and respect for tradition – evident in the snacks and wine-tasting before the meal. Ask for recommendations, but, if there are fresh porcini mushrooms on offer, just let them do their thing! Breathtaking vintage wine cellar.
Campo San Lorenzo 14.
Tel: (0984) 579 026.
www.latavernetta.info

Horse riding
Salvatore comes recommended, offering lessons and leading excursions through the

Sila countryside on horseback.
Tel: 360 283 252.
Skiing
Sci Al Baita (*Tel: 338 309 6063*) offers skiing tuition, and there are also skiing and snowboarding excursions available with private **professional guides** (*Tel: 349 107 8789*). The **Pro Loco** tourist office (*Tel: (0984) 579 159*) also has information on skiing and snowboarding, as well as trekking and hiring guides.

Castrovillari
La Locanda di Alia ★★★
The accommodation here runs somewhat in second place to the restaurant, which is conceivably the only reason to stay here. The motel-type rooms vary in configuration, but are an odd mix of styles and suggest questionable maintenance, unlike the lovely garden and pool, which appear to attract most of the attention.
Via Ietticelli.
Tel: (0981) 463 70.
www.alia.it

Eating out

La Locanda di Alia ★★★★

Once considered one of the best eating places in Calabria, these days it appears that this elegant restaurant is a bit of a hit-and-miss affair. The food is rustic, hearty, sometimes inventive, but presentation is mired in the early 1990s, when the restaurant garnered its reputation. It's always been an unlikely gastronomic destination, once because of the location, now, sadly, because of the uneven food and questionable service.
Via Ietticelli.
Tel: (0981) 463 70.
www.alia.it

Cosenza

Accommodation

Royal Hotel ★

A good, clean hotel in a handy location right around the corner from the main shopping street and ten minutes from the old town. The friendly staff speak English.
Via Molinella 24e.
Tel: (0984) 412 165.
www.hotelroyalsas.it

Vescovo Rosso ★★

This bright and cheerful modern hotel is in the city centre, conveniently placed for exploring the old town. All rooms have a terrace and there's also a self-catering apartment. The on-site restaurant is popular, too.
Viale della Repubblica 21.
Tel: (0984) 718 82.
www.vescovorosso.com

Eating out

Basilico ★

One of the few late openers in the commercial centre of town, this modest pizza place does fantastic pizzas, a great antipasto plate and good, cheap house wines – very popular with locals.
Via Panebianco 34s.
Tel: (0984) 408 529.

Calabria Bella ★

Next to the Duomo, this very traditional restaurant is handily placed for lunch after sightseeing. Pleasant outdoor seating, local dishes and good antipasti.
Piazza Duomo.
Tel: (0984) 793 531.

Taverna L'Arco Vecchio ★★

Worth seeking out, this unassuming but endearing little taverna does remarkable fresh handmade pasta dishes such as gnocchi.
Piazza Archi di Ciacco 21.
Tel: (0984) 725 64.

Entertainment

Gran Caffè Renzelli ★

The best place in the old town for *aperitivi* or coffee is this very charming, elegant, old-style grand café one block from the Duomo, with seating on a sunny terrace out front and, in the atmospheric interior, the aroma of great coffee.
Cnr Corso Telesio.
www.grancafferenzelli.it

Sport and leisure

Orme nel Parco

This superb outdoor tour organisation runs a wide range of excellent walking, trekking and 4WD excursions into the Sila, Pollino and

Aspromonte mountain ranges and national parks.
Viale Crotone 210, Catanzaro Lido.
Tel: (0961) 731 290.
www.ormenelparco.it

Diamante
ACCOMMODATION
Ferretti Hotel ★★★
Open from May to September, this is very much your Calabrian summer resort, with a private beach, swimming pool, tennis courts and other sports facilities. The rooms are comfortable and have private terraces.
Via Poseidone 1.
Tel: (0985) 814 28.
www.ferrettihotel.it

EATING OUT
Taverna del Pescatore ★★
This smart fish restaurant, with views over the port, serves excellent seafood antipasti and mains. They also do great pizza for those who don't love the fruits of the sea.
Via Calvario.
Tel: (0985) 814 82.

SPORT AND LEISURE
Diamante and the surrounding beaches have the usual plethora of summer lidos.

Morano Calabro
ACCOMMODATION
Villa San Domenico ★★
A very charming and elegant hotel set in a large old stone palazzo with splendid views over the lower town and out to the valley. The warren of alleyways of the upper town is right behind the hotel, so it's handily placed for exploring. There's a lovely garden and terrace, and parking.
Via Sotto gli Olmi.
Tel: (0981) 399 991/881.
www.
albergovillasandomenico.it

EATING OUT
Villa San Domenico ★★
The atmospheric dining rooms and traditional cuisine are a highlight here. There's no menu – just dishes of the day, made from the freshest of local produce, as well as decent house wine. Very popular with locals for a

weekend lunch.
Via Sotto gli Olmi.
Tel: (0981) 399 991/881.
www.
albergovillasandomenico.it

Rossano
ACCOMMODATION
Hotel Scigliano ★★
This decent three-star hotel is modern and centrally located and has a good restaurant.
Viale Margherita 257.
Tel: (0983) 511 846.
www.hotelscigliano.it

EATING OUT
Per Bacco ★
This wine bar and restaurant on the Duomo square has great local dishes and wines as well as jazz and blues.
Piazza Duomo 21/23.
Tel: (0983) 520 299.

La Tavernetta Antica ★★
A characterful little taverna specialising in typical Calabrian dishes. Try their antipasti.
Via Prigioni 40.
Tel: (0983) 522 778.

CROTONE PROVINCE
Crotone
ACCOMMODATION
Palazzo Foti Hotel ★★★
A fresh, modern, four-

star hotel overlooking the waterfront promenade, its rooms are spacious and comfortable, but be sure to ask for one with a sea view. They do a decent breakfast with great coffee (the terrace café is popular with locals). Friendly staff and secure parking (a must in this city).

Via Cristoforo Colombo 79.
Tel: (0962) 900 608.
www.palazzofoti.it

Lido degli Scogli ★★★★
This comfortable four-star resort is right on the beach and boasts a big swimming pool, disco and fine restaurant. This is a good choice for those who want to spend more time in the water than out.

Viale Magna Grecia 49.
Tel: (0962) 255 49.
www.lidodegliscogli.com

EATING OUT
Da Ercole ★★
This is a renowned Crotone seafood eatery where the chef (a bit of a local celebrity) bobs from table to table

ensuring that the guests are enjoying the endless seafood feast. You can order from the menu or let the chef do his thing – we recommend the latter. It's an endearingly old-fashioned experience. The *crudo antipasti* (raw seafood plate) and the *linguine a pitagora* (a type of sea anemone) are noteworthy.

Viale Gramsci 122.
Tel: (0962) 901 425.
www.daercole.com

Casa di Rosa ★★★
Sumptuous seafood is the calling card of this restaurant – and it delivers in spades. Forget about the Italian staples and instead sample interesting local dishes such as spaghetti with *bottarga* (dried tuna roe) and the popular fish *ragù*.

Via Cristoforo Colombo 117.
Tel: (0962) 219 46.

Ristorante Lido degli Scogli ★★★
Another local favourite for its fresh seafood is this restaurant at the Lido degli Scogli resort. Expect refined

preparation of local fish (check the house specials), a good wine list and panoramic views.

Viale Magna Grecia 49.
Tel: (0962) 255 49.
www.lidodegliscogli.com

La Sosta da Marcello ★★★
Another elegant restaurant where fresh local seafood gets the attention it deserves; *misto affumicato di pesce spada e tonno* (smoked swordfish and tuna) and *risotto al pescatore* (risotto with fish) are just two of the superb dishes on offer.

Via E di Bartolo 20/22.
Tel: (0962) 238 31.
www.lasostadamarcello.it

ENTERTAINMENT
The city hosts numerous concerts, dance parties and festivals during summer. Check with your hotel or the tourist office to see what's on while you're in town.

Teatro Apollo
This theatre is the venue for a wide variety of

concerts and musical performances from orchestras to jazz and is part of the famous Teatro Stabile di Calabria group.
Via Regina Margherita 7. Tel: (0962) 905 416. www. teatrostabilecalabria.it

SPORT AND LEISURE
Hera Sub Diving Center
The area is noted for its diving, and this centre hosts snorkelling trips and open-water diving excursions for the more experienced divers.
Largo Cristoforo Colombo 8. Tel: 347 380 0856.

Capo Rizzuto and Le Castella
ACCOMMODATION
Baia degli Dei ★★
With rooms facing the Aragonese Castle, this is a large beach resort with great views. Well equipped, it boasts a private beach, swimming pool and gardens, fitness club and beauty centre, as well as good facilities for children. It's a fantastic choice for family getaways for a few days.

Le Castella. Tel: (0962) 795 235/642. www.baiadeglidei.com

EATING OUT
Ristorante Micomare ★★
This is a good local restaurant with a terrace overlooking the sea and castle. The emphasis of the Micomare's short menu is on fresh seafood and Calabrian specialities as well as Italian staples.
Via Vittoria 7, Le Castella. Tel: (0962) 795 082.

ENTERTAINMENT
There are plenty of café-bars and *gelaterie* opposite the castle and in the streets on and around the waterfront. There are also some decidedly dodgy pubs and clubs around the port area. Regular dance parties are held in dedicated spaces and on resort beaches during summer, so look for posters or check with your hotel.

SPORT AND LEISURE
Aquarium
This aquarium at

Capo Rizzuto sees more school groups than tourists visiting its informative exhibitions on local sea life. However, it's worthwhile dropping in if you have some spare time and are intrigued by the archaeological treasures beneath the sea as much as the marine life.
Piazza del Santuario. Tel: (0962) 796 029. www. riservamarinacaporizzuto. it
Le Cannella
This diving centre offers diving and snorkelling excursions. Note that, because of the undersea treasures still to be discovered in ancient wrecks that can be found in the area, many places are zoned and cannot be dived without going through a company such as Le Cannella.
Tel: (0962) 799 969. www.lecannella.com
Fishing
Fishing is allowed only in zoned areas. For sport-fishing trips, go to the marina.

174

Index

A

Accademia Cosentina 81
accommodation 130–31
agriculture 8, 38, 109
air travel 150
Alberti family 43
Altomonte 90–91
Amantea 21, 84–5
Amarelli Fabbrica di
    Liquirizia 98–9
aquarium 117
archaeological remains
    29–30, 35, 45, 55, 74,
    95–7, 111, 112, 114–15,
    116, 117–18
architecture 32, 34, 35, 50,
    56–7, 62, 71, 81, 91, 99,
    112
Area Marina Protetta Capo
    Rizzuto 116–17
Aspromonte National Park
    8, 21, 48–9, 120, 121–2
Athena Promachos 35
ATMs 150

B

Bagaladi 44, 48
Bagnara Calabra 38
ballet 139
bars 138–9
baths 35
beaches 8, 38, 52, 60–61,
    64, 73, 87, 126, 147
Belmonte Calabro 85
Belvedere Marittimo 86–7
Benassai, Giuseppe 31
bergamot 143
birds 93
Bivongi 50
Bosnian pine 7, 93
Bova Marina 44
bowling alleys 149

C

cafés 134–5, 136
Calabria–Sicily bridge 13
Camigliatello Silano 21,
    102–3, 107, 147
Cannizzaro, Vincenzo 31
Capo Colonna 117–18
Capo Rizzuto 116–19
Capo Vaticano 52, 64
car hire 122, 123–4, 128
Carolei 85
Carpitella, Diego 17
Casalnuovo 124
Castello Aragonese (Capo
    Rizzuto) 117–18
Castello Aragonese (Reggio
    di Calabria) 33–4
Castello Carlo V 111, 113
Castello Ruffo 38
Castello Svevo (Cosenza)
    82
castles 33–4, 38, 54–5, 65,

71–2, 82, 84, 98, 111,
    113, 118–19
Castrovillari 92–3
Catanoso, Padre Gaetano
    42
Catanzaro 6, 70–72
Catanzaro province 70–73
cathedrals 22, 34, 47, 50,
    56–7, 62, 71, 72, 81, 82,
    99, 113
Cattedrale (Crotone) 113
Cattedrale dell'Assunta
    (Gerace) 47
Cedri Riviera 86–7
Cefaly, Andrea 31
ceramics 74–5, 86–7,
    140–42
Charles I of Anjou 10–11
Chiesa e Convento di San
    Domenico (Cosenza)
    79, 81, 82
Chiesa e Convento di Santa
    Maria delle Vergini 83
Chiesa del Gesù 62–3
Chiesa dell'Immacolata
    (Crotone) 112
Chiesa dell'Immacolata
    (Pizzo) 65
Chiesa e Monasterio di
    Santa Maria Nuova
    Odigitria 83
Chiesa degli Ottimati 34
Chiesa del Sacro Cuore
    (Gerace) 47
Chiesa di San Bernardino
    90
Chiesa San Domenico
    (Stilo) 50
Chiesa San Francesco
    (Stilo) 50
Chiesa di San Francesco
    d'Assisi (Cosenza) 83
Chiesa di San Francesco
    d'Assisi (Gerace) 47
Chiesa San Giovanni 50
Chiesa di San Giuseppe
    112
Chiesa di Santa Caterina 62
Chiesa di Santa Maria
    Assunta 94
Chiesa di Santa Maria della
    Consolazione 91
Chiesa di Santi Pietro e
    Paolo (Morano
    Calabro) 90
Chiesa del Santissimo
    Rosario 71
Chiesa SS Apostoli Pietro e
    Paolo (Pedace) 106
Chiesetta di Piedigrotta
    65
children 148–9
chilli peppers 88, 132,
    141–2
Chorio 42, 48

churches 23, 56, 57 *see also
    individual terms*
cinema 139
Citrus Coast 86–7
Civita 94–5
climate 108, 126, 127, 148,
    156
clubs 139
Condofuri 124
consulates 157
Convento delle
    Cappuccinelle 82
Convento di San Francesco
    d'Assisi (Castrovillari)
    93
convents 58–9, 63, 79, 81,
    82–3, 93
conversion tables 151
Cortale 73
Cosenza 76–83
Cosenza province 76–87,
    90–99, 102–7
credit cards 150
crime 11, 13, 36–7, 38, 109,
    156
Crotone 110–13, 116
Crotone province 110–13,
    116–19
culture 14–17 *see also
    individual terms*
customs regulations 150
cycling 144

D

debit cards 150
Diamante 87
disabilities 153
diving 144
Domanico 85
Douglas, Norman 100,
    152
dress 133
driving 22, 23, 24, 25, 48–9,
    66, 72, 85, 106–7,
    122–4, 128–9, 130,
    150
Duomo (Catanzaro) 71
Duomo (Cosenza) 81, 82
Duomo (Reggio) 34, 56–7
Duomo (Rossano) 99
Duomo (Stilo) 50
Duomo (Tropea) 62

E

earthquakes 8, 34, 43, 56
eating out 22, 60, 62, 65,
    92, 133–5, 136, 138,
    148, 151
economy 14–15, 108–9
electricity 150
embassies 157
embroidery 75
emergencies 156–7
emigration 37, 103, 107,
    109

entertainment 136–9 *see
    also* eating out;
    passeggiata
events 16, 18–19, 50, 73,
    90–91, 136

F

fashion 38
fauna 7–8, 93, 104, 117, 120
ferries 150
festivals 16, 18, 19, 50,
    90–91
flora 7, 26, 42–3, 48, 66, 85,
    93, 105, 117, 120–21
folk music 16–17
folklore and myths 15–16,
    42, 59, 86
food and drink 68, 88–9,
    132–5, 142–3 *see also
    individual terms*
football 144–5
forests 66–7, 104
Francesco di Paola, San 86

G

Galati 45
galleries 30–31, 33, 35, 113,
    116
Gambarie 49
gardens 34, 81, 82
Garibaldi, Giuseppe 108
gelaterie 32, 62, 65, 136, 138
Gerace 46–7, 57
ghost towns 42–4, 48
Gimigliano 72
Gioia Tauro 38
Giuseppe de Nava statue 32
Grand Tour 100–101, 107
guides 93, 94, 121–2, 146

H

handicrafts 70, 72, 73,
    74–5, 86–7, 140–42
health 148, 151, 152, 156
hikes 93, 94, 102–3, 120,
    121–2, 145–7
hill towns 21 *see also
    individual terms*
history 10–11, 28, 40–41,
    52–3, 59, 70, 78, 84,
    108–9, 110, 114–15
horse riding 147
hotels 130

I

ice cream 32, 62, 65, 136,
    138
Il Castello Normanno-
    Svevo (Vibo Valentia)
    54–5
Il Castello di San Angelo 98
Il Codex Purpureus 57, 99
Il Monumento ai Caduti 33
Il Piccolo Museo San Paolo
    30

insurance 156
Internet 150
Ionian coast 44–6
itineraries 22–5

K
kitesurfing 147

L
L'Arena dello Stretto 35
L'Isola Bella 58–9, 63
L'Oratorio del San Marco 98
La Cattolica di Stilo 50–51, 56
La Certosa di Serra San Bruno 66–7, 68
La Costa Viola 38–9
La Mura Greche 35
La Nave della Sila 103, 107
La Pinocoteca Civica (Reggio) 30–31, 33
La Villa Comunale (Reggio) 34
Laganadi 49
Lago 85, 124
Lago Ampollino 104, 106
Lago Arvo 104, 106
Lago Cecita 105, 107
language 6, 40, 94–5, 154–5
Le Castella (Capo Rizzuto) 118–19
Le Terme Romane 35
library (Cosenza) 81
lifestyle 14–15, 17, 27, 54, 60, 63, 67, 78, 85, 108, 109, 110–11, 124–5, 136–9
liquorice 98–9, 143
Locri 45
Locri Epizefiri 45, 114
Lorica 104, 106

M
Mafia 11, 13, 36–7, 38, 109
Mar Piccolo 60–61
Mare Grande 60–61
Marina di Gioiosa Jonica 45–6
marine life 8, 117
marine and nature park 116–17
markets 87, 135
medical aid 151, 152, 156
metalwork 74, 75
Mezzogiorno 6, 108–9
monasteries 44, 48, 66–7, 68, 98
Monastero di San Angel 44, 48
money 150
Montealto 48
Montebello family 43
Monumento all'Italia 33
Morano Calabro 21, 90, 92
Murat Castle 65
Museo Archeologico Nazionale (Crotone) 111, 112, 115, 116

Museo Archeologico Nazionale Vito Capialbi 55
Museo Arte Contemporanea (MACK) 113, 116
Museo della Certosa 68
Museo Diocesano (Rossano) 57, 99
Museo Etnico Arbëresh 95
Museo Nazionale Archeologico della Sibaritide 97
Museo Nazionale di Reggio Calabria 21, 29–30, 32, 115
Museo del Parco Archeologico di Capo Colonna 116, 118–19
museums 21, 29–31, 32, 33, 55, 57, 68, 95, 97, 98–9, 103, 107, 111, 112, 113, 114, 115, 116–18
music 16–17, 136, 139

N
'Ndrangheta 11, 13, 36–7, 38, 109
'nduja (sausage meat) 88–9
nightlife 139

O
opening hours 134, 135, 150–51
opera 139

P
palazzi 21, 84–5, 98, 112, 113
Palazzo Barracco 113
Palazzo delle Clarisse 84–5
Palmi 38
Paola 86
Parchi Letterari 101, 107
Parco Nazionale dell'Aspromonte 8, 21, 48–9, 120–2
Parco Nazionale del Pollino 7, 93, 94, 120, 122–3
Parco Nazionale della Sila 7–8, 102–7, 120, 121–2, 123
Parco Old Calabria 101, 107
parking 130
parks 7–8, 21, 48–9, 93, 94, 101, 102–7, 116–18, 120–23, 145–7
passeggiata 17, 27, 54, 60, 67, 85, 136
passports 151
Pedace 106
Pentedattilo 42–4, 48
people 6, 40, 41, 94–5
peperoncini (chilli peppers) 88, 132, 141–2
pharmacies 151, 152
pine trees 7, 93, 105
Pizzo 21, 52, 64–5, 140, 143

police 156
politics 11, 12–13
Pollino National Park 7, 93, 94, 120, 122–3
post 152
Potame 85, 124
pottery 74–5, 86–7, 140–42
Praia a Mare 87
preserved food 89, 104
Preti, Mattia 31
psychics 86
public holidays 152
public transport 129, 150

R
reading 101, 152
real estate 27
Reggio di Calabria 28–35, 139
Reggio di Calabria province 26–35, 38–9, 42–51
religion 6, 16, 41
reserves 105, 116–17
restaurants 22, 60, 92, 133, 135, 138, 148, 151
Riace bronzes 28, 29
Riserva Naturale I Giganti della Sila 105
Roccella Jonica 46
Roghudi 44, 124
Rossano 57, 97–9

S
safety 66, 72, 121, 123, 128, 148, 156
sailing 147
St Bruno's Pond 69
Salazar, Demetrio 31
San Alessio 49
San Demetrio Corone 125
San Floro 73
San Giovannello (Gerace) 47
San Giovanni in Fiore 106–7
San Pietro Apostolo 72
Santa Maria dell'Isola 58–9, 63
Santa Severina 125
santine (psychics) 86
Santuario di San Francesco di Paola 57
Santuario di Santa Maria nel Bosco 66–7, 68–9
sausage meat 88–9
Scilla 21, 38–9
sea travel 150
seafood 85, 89, 132
seasons 126–7
Serra San Bruno 66–9
Serrastretta 72
shipwreck 119
shopping 135, 140–43, 150–51
Sibari 95–7
Siderno 46
silk 70, 73, 75
skiing 103, 147

smoking 152
Soverato 73
sport and activity 93, 94, 102–3, 120, 121–2, 127, 144–7, 148–9
Squillace 72
Staiti 124
Stilo 50–51, 56
Strait of Messina 6
straw and wicker products 75, 140
students 78

T
tax 152
Teatro Comunale Francesco Cilea 32–3
telephones 152–3
Terrati 124
textiles 70, 72, 73, 75, 140
theatre 139
time 153
tipping 135
Tiriolo 72
toilets 153
Torre Camigliati 101, 107
trains 129, 150
Tropea 21, 52, 58–63, 140–41, 143
Tropea onion 60
Tyrrhenian coast 86–7

V
vegetarian food 132
Versace, Gianni 38
Vibo Valentia 53–5
Vibo Valentia Marina 54
Vibo Valentia province 52–5, 58–69
Villa Berlingieri 112
Villa Genoese Zerbi 35
Villa Vecchia (Cosenza) 81, 82
Violet Coast 38–9
visas 151

W
walks 32–5, 59–60, 62–3, 82–3, 112–13 see also hikes; passeggiata
water, spring 66
water parks 149
windsurfing 147
wine 21, 40, 118, 139
woodwork 75

Acknowledgements

Thomas Cook Publishing wishes to thank TERRY CARTER, to whom the copyright belongs, for the photographs in this book, except for the following images:

DREAMSTIME.COM 1, 102 (Massimo Valicchia), 133 (Gennaro Carbone)
GETTY IMAGES 137 (Vincenzo Lombardo)
ISTOCKPHOTO 88 (SeanShot)
PICTURES COLOUR LIBRARY 131
PHOTOSHOT 134 (Dionisio Iemma)
WIKIMEDIA COMMONS 68, 69 (Marcuscalabresus)
WORLD PICTURES/PHOTOSHOT 45, 108, 109
WWW.FLICKR.COM 37 (Fabrizio Sinopoli), 95 (Peter Stewart)

For CAMBRIDGE PUBLISHING MANAGEMENT LIMITED:
Project editor: Jennifer Jahn
Copy editor: Anne McGregor
Typesetter: Trevor Double
Proofreaders: Jan McCann & Karolin Thomas
Indexer: Karolin Thomas

SEND YOUR THOUGHTS TO
BOOKS@THOMASCOOK.COM

We're committed to providing the very best up-to-date information in our travel guides and constantly strive to make them as useful as they can be. You can help us to improve future editions by letting us have your feedback. If you've made a wonderful discovery on your travels that we don't already feature, if you'd like to inform us about recent changes to anything that we do include, or if you simply want to let us know your thoughts about this guidebook and how we can make it even better – we'd love to hear from you.

Send us ideas, discoveries and recommendations today and then look out for your valuable input in the next edition of this title.

Emails to the above address, or letters to the traveller guides Series Editor, Thomas Cook Publishing, PO Box 227, Coningsby Road, Peterborough PE3 8SB, UK.

Please don't forget to let us know which title your feedback refers to!